A Marriage in Our Time

When believer meets non-believer

ANITA DOWSING

A Marriage in Our Time

When believer meets non-believer

Sheed & Ward

London

ISBN 0 7220 5261 8

Published in Great Britain in 2000 by
Sheed & Ward Limited
4 Rickett Street
London SW6 1RU

Edit, design, typesetting: Bill Ireson
Printed in Great Britain by
Biddles Limited, Guildford and King's Lynn

For Roy

Men who are enablers of their wives' ventures become
partners in their adventures.
    Dolores S. Lecky, *The Ordinary Way: A Family Spirituality*

Contents

Acknowledgements

The people who have helped make this book possible are many. They range from those who read the manuscript, to those who inspired me through their own work, to those who prayed for me (and believed in me!). They also include those who taught me the reality of publishing a book today and those who simply said something encouraging, just when I needed it. I would like to thank them all for the help they have given me.

Those who read the book in manuscript have all made their contributions to its final form. Father Neil Crayden, who encouraged my first, tentative, suggestion that I should write a book on marriage between a Christian and a non-believer, continued to encourage and comment, as I wrote. Frances Taylor of Catholic Marriage Care, shared her own experience and her experience as a marriage counsellor with me, thereby enabling me to see marriage through eyes other than my own. Cynthia Robinson read the manuscript from the point of view of a married woman in comparable circumstances to mine and also as someone with a wide experience in journalism, social work and work with traumatised women. All three have supplemented my limited field of vision with their own and hence immensely enriched the book.

My debt to Margaret Spufford is great, both as a historian who helped provide a context for my writing and as a fellow 'sharer-of-her-story' – without her book *Celebration*, mine would not have been written.

Dolores Lecky's book about marriage and family life, *The Ordinary Way: A Family Spirituality*, I have read and re-read many times over the years and it has taught me much about ways of living a marriage where both partners are Catholics. While I was writing about my own, very different, situation, I often took her book as the starting point for my reflection.

Two writers have helped me understand better the reality of getting a book published. At the beginning of my journey, Bruce Robinson warned me of the hardness of the road ahead (and gave me some tips too!) and, towards its conclusion, Ruth Burrows (Sister Rachel of Quidenham) encouraged me and taught me perseverance.

Many people have prayed for me and with me, as I wrote the book. I am particularly grateful to Father Chris Dyckhoff, S J, who spared the time, and Ruth Burrows, who accompanied me in prayer and practicality.

I would like to thank all the people, whether living or dead, whether they knew it or not, who have helped guide me in the writing and publication of this book.

The publishers join with me in thanking the following for permission to quote from the copyright works listed:

Burns & Oates Ltd: Columba Cary–Elwes, *Work and Prayer*.
Crossroads Publishing: Dolores S. Lecky, *The Ordinary Way: A Family Spirituality*.
Darton, Longman & Todd Ltd: Karl Rahner, *Theological Investigations*, Volume VI (passages also contained in *A Rahner Reader*).
Faber & Faber Ltd: W. H. Auden, 'Sext', *Collected Shorter Poems 1927–57*.
HarperCollins Religious: Sheila Cassidy, *Audacity to Believe*.

ANITA DOWSING
July 2000

CHAPTER ONE

Beginnings

. . . to desire 'unlimited' good for another person is really to desire God for that person.

Karol Wojtyla (Pope John Paul II)[1]

Theology should begin when the sun sets – after the experiences of the day.

Gustave Gutierrez[2]

This book has been a long time in the writing, or rather, in the thinking. When, over the years, friends have encouraged me to write about marriage, I have always held back. I felt that, as a Christian (Roman Catholic) married to a non-believer, I did not have sufficient experience of *Christian* marriage.

Marriage, any marriage, implies an open-ended commitment. For me, sharing every day of my life with a man who does not believe in God presents me with very practical questions about how I am meant to *do* this sharing: 'What words do I choose to talk about my faith? (Do I talk about it at all?). How do I fit prayer into my marriage? What do I do about going to church? And when I am in church, how do I deal with the inevitable pain of being there alone, as a "single" person?'[3] This pain is, of course, not mine alone. My husband is also 'single', in this respect.[4]

If I was going to write a book about marriage, I needed to see at least the beginning of some answers to the questions that I face every day and for a long time there did not seem to be any answers that satisfied *me*. So I stalled, or, rather, I began to look at other topics. While I was considering the idea of a book on spirituality, I went to see a friend, who is interested in such topics. 'Perhaps she will give me a clue (unknowingly!),' I thought. As we walked along the river near her house, on a lovely spring morning, she said, 'Why don't you write about marriage?'

To my dismay this sounded, and felt, very much like the 'word' I had been waiting for, but I did not know what to do with it. I therefore carried on (somewhat pigheadedly) with my plans for a book on spirituality, until a publisher told me that someone else was writing on that topic. It seemed that I was being guided towards writing a book that I could not write.

'Normal' marriage

The teaching of the Catholic Church about marriage takes as its starting point, and norm, marriage between two Catholics.[5] It has regulations for 'mixed marriages' (that is, those with Christians of other denominations) and for marriages involving 'disparity of cult' (that is, between a Catholic and a non-baptised person). However, it seems that the Church has very little to say (that I am aware of) about marriage with a non-believer, who may or may not have been baptised.[6] Yet in today's world, certainly in the West, this situation appears to be very common and not only in the Catholic Church. On hearing the subject of my book, a vicar's wife said to me, 'This must be the most common situation today. I see so many "single" people in church.'

About the 'non-believing partner' in a marriage, one sometimes hears, 'But why don't you just bring him/her to the parish social?' Quite apart from the question of whether 'he/she' *wants* to go to the parish social, there is the question of whether it is enough. 'Singleness', in religious matters, runs through the whole of such a marriage. If there is to be any kind of answer to the question of how to live such a marriage in a way that attempts to share the religious dimension too, attending the parish social is only going to be a very small part of it.

So I carried on thinking – and observing – what was actually happening in my own marriage. A comment made by a priest struck a chord with me. About the practicalities of living married life, he said, 'We owe so much to the non-believing partners who give moral and practical support to their Catholic wives or husbands, faithfully, year after year.' This was another dimension to my situation, and one that stressed *togetherness*.

I work in adult religious education for the Catholic Church. This provides me with many opportunities to speak to others in the same situation as my own. Two themes stand out in these conversations: first, the 'open-ended' pain (and challenge) of what cannot be shared; and, second, the joy of support – almost an act of faith – given by someone who does not understand what he/she is supporting.

'Celebration'

In 1989 I visited my friend, Margaret Spufford. Shortly afterwards, her book *Celebration* was published. In it she describes a life of both pain and joy: the pain of watching her terminally ill daughter get worse and of living with a painful bone disease herself, but also the joy of an exceptionally creative and fruitful life.[7] It struck me that there were significant similarities between our situations.

Margaret was writing from within pain and from within an unresolved situation. Her circumstances spoke to my (very different) circumstances: the story of my marriage – and any marriage where faith cannot be shared – is, like hers, a story of living with a painful, and unresolved situation. It is also a story of the challenge presented by these circumstances and of unexpected and surprising joys. The theme of pain interwoven with joy that I had began to see as an essential part of my marriage was being lit up from a new angle.

The 'anonymous Christian'

Some time after I had been to see Margaret, I began to read the works of Karl Rahner, the German Jesuit theologian. Here I first encountered Rahner's concept of the *anonymous Christian*, the person who, unknowingly, follows Christ by trying to do all that is right, but who does not believe in Christ – or God.

The 'open-endedness' of Margaret Spufford's story together with Rahner's concept of the anonymous Christian were to provide major 'keys' to my *Christian* understanding of my marriage. One further key was needed before I could begin to write this book.

During his visit to the UK in 1982, Pope John Paul II said that in a marriage between Christians of different denominations the partners live the hopes and difficulties of the path to unity.[8] He did not mention those people who are married to non-believers, but when I read his words some years later, it struck me that, just as an inter-church marriage reflected the relationship between the churches, so a marriage between a Christian and a non-believer mirrored the link between the Roman Catholic Church and the world.

With these three 'keys' – the open-endedness of not sharing faith, the theology of the anonymous Christian, and the parallel with the Church and the world – I now felt equipped to write the book I had been thinking about for so long.

All three 'keys' provide a kind of 'bridge' to non-belief. The anonymous Christian is already a follower of Christ without knowing it and so can share 'practice', though not faith, with a believing spouse. Scriptural references and Church teaching on the relationship between the Church and the world are part of the setting for such a marriage and so are the open-endedness of an unresolved situation accompanied by both pain and joy, as described by Margaret Spufford.

My story

So, I set out to write 'my story and my story with my husband' as a case study in the hope that it would be of help to others in the same situation. It is written from my point of view, but with the blessing, and encouragement, of my husband. As the sub-title of this book suggests, the story concentrates on our attempts, and failures, to bridge the religious divide between us. It tells of the growing together of two very different people – to the differences in religion were added differences in nationality (I was born in Denmark), in academic subject (the science/arts divide), and also in social background.

As I wrote, I came to realise that the difficulty of not sharing something central to one partner in a marriage also affects the 'non-sharing' partner. My husband's pain at being outside and being unable to understand my religious practice is very real. The generosity of his support is all the more remarkable and I have tried to describe the view, as seen through his eyes, in Chapter Two.

Definition of subject

This book is, then, a case study. This implies a specific focus and, inevitably, the associated limitations. I have described the areas where my husband and I have had difficulties in sharing, because of the difference in belief between us. I have also described the gradual growing together (in spite of, or rather in and through, those difficulties) which has taken place over the years. I have therefore not given a complete picture of our marriage, but only of those aspects which seem directly relevant to the subject.

Some areas, such as the Roman Catholic Church's teaching on

sexual morality, which might have been expected to present problems in such a marriage, have in fact not been a cause of difficulty, and have therefore not been included.

My limitations

One of my reservations about writing this book has concerned my lack of formal theological training. I began adult life as a linguist and, although I now work for the Catholic Church in a voluntary capacity, my knowledge of theology has been 'picked up along the way'. In understanding the theology of Karl Rahner it took some encouraging words from a priest before I felt ready to make use of what I had learnt. When I protested that I was not an expert, he simply said, 'This is what helped you, so use it!'

It is a necessary part of my story that it be set in the context of the Roman Catholic teaching and spiritual writing from Catholic and other Christian sources that have helped direct me. While writing this book, I have been struck by how often the material I needed to write the next chapter, has, somehow, appeared on my doorstep.

Vocabulary

I have given much thought to the use of the terms *Christian* and (Roman) *Catholic*. Much of what I say would, I think, be true of all Christians married to non-believers, but as a Roman Catholic I obviously write from within a particular tradition and in the context of the teaching of the Roman Catholic Church.

As a general principle, I have used the word *Christian* where its use applies to all Christians. I have used the term (Roman) *Catholic* where I refer to that Church or where it is necessary to distinguish between (Roman) *Catholics* and other *Christians*. As *Roman Catholic* is an unwieldy term, I have mostly used *Catholic*, only adding *Roman* for clarity, or variety.

I have spoken about being married to a *non-believer*, which seems a very negative way of describing someone. However, other terms which I considered, such as *atheist* or *agnostic* seem equally negative and have narrower meanings than non-believer. *Humanist*, although more positive, suggests allegiance to a 'religion' or system of thought without God; again, a much narrower definition than non-believer and one which would not apply to my husband. In spite of its deficiencies, I have therefore used the term non-believer about people who do not believe in God.

Experience

My story is, then, based on my own experience, but experience set in the context of theological and spiritual writing. It therefore invites dialogue with theology. Canon Vanstone has stressed the importance of experience as a way of throwing light on theology – just as theology lights up experience:

> One longs to hear from experience 'knocking at the door' of theology and demanding to be let in – not necessarily to challenge theological propositions but also to illuminate or confirm them.[9]

As suggested by Gutierrez in the quotation at the beginning of this chapter, the conclusions of this book have been reached, 'at sunset' – after prayer, reflection and conversation with others.

Who is this book for?

I hope this book will help other people – and those trying to help them – in the same situation as mine. It is not only for Christians married to people who do not believe in God and for those who do not believe but do feel baffled by the strange and, seemingly, inaccessible world of faith. The book is also addressed to clergy, who help prepare couples for marriage (and who reflect on the theology of marriage), to marriage counsellors and couples who assist them – and, I hope, that couples who are thinking about marriage or preparing for it will read it too. To them, especially, I would like to quote the comment of a priest who read the book in manuscript. 'You and your husband have far more in common than you think!'

***

My husband encouraged me to write this book on 30 December 1994, the Feast of the Holy Family, at the end of the Year of the Family, and so I began.

CHAPTER TWO

Looking in From the Outside

... the proclaiming West can itself become more Christian by having to listen in order to become more comprehensible.
Karl Rahner[1]

What we can understand of [loving God] is but a fraction of the mystery; and yet it is not right we should refrain from speaking about the very little that we can take in.
St Bernard of Clairvaux[2]

When we married, my husband gave me a cross, as a sign that he would never come between me and the Church. I have worn that cross ever since and to me it summarises his whole attitude to my religion.

My husband knows that the cross is the central part of my life, or rather, it is what underpins and informs all aspects of my life. He is prepared to do everything he can to support me, but he does see himself as an onlooker – and, sometimes, from the sidelines, as a supporter and commentator.

Meeting a Catholic

We first began to go out together at about the time when Jackie Kennedy, widow of the murdered President John F. Kennedy, married the divorced shipping magnate Aristotle Onassis.

Their marriage was much in the news, so it is not surprising that we talked about it and the religious implications, one of the very first times we had a meal out together. I can still see myself in the restaurant, feeling a bit shy and awkward that the subject of religion had come up so early, before we had really had time to get to know each other. I suppose I must have had an inkling of how important this conversation (and indeed this relationship!) was going to be – or I would not now have remembered it.

I said something like: 'I can't understand how Jackie Kennedy as a Roman Catholic can marry someone who is divorced and his wife still living. For Catholics marriage is for life, you see. I don't understand how can she do it!'[3] I probably said that I could not imagine doing something like that, as it would mean that I could not go to communion any longer and so not take part fully in the life of my Church. It was this legal aspect and the thought of being excluded from communion that struck me at the time. I had, as yet, had very little experience in human relationships.

On the other hand, the young man I had so recently got to know saw the human situation and said, 'She may have been looking for safety. Remember, her brother-in-law (Robert Kennedy], who I think she has relied on a good deal for support since her husband was killed, was assassinated not so long ago. She may have had as much as she can take. For the moment, anyway, she may need to feel secure more than anything else.'

By then, of course, it had become clear that I was a Catholic (and a very legalistic one) and that he was . . . not a Catholic. (I was later to learn that, though baptised as an Anglican, he had never believed in God.) In a sense, this conversation set the 'scene' for our whole relationship. I had stated a principle, without thinking much about the people involved. He saw the human situation – the 'circumstances' that might have led people to act the way they did. This conversation, too, showed, at a very early stage, that if our relationship was to develop, my religion and his attitude to it would be a crucial factor.

It is only in retrospect that I realise that our conversation also showed that his questions could lead me to reflect more carefully about the reasons why I kept to certain rules of behaviour. They were in fact an invitation to live at a deeper level than before.

Preparing to get married

I met my husband while we were both doing research at the University of Keele in Staffordshire, he in physics, I in English language. We got engaged and, as I still had my MA dissertation to write at the University of Copenhagen, the plan was for me to return to Denmark for one year before we married. Later, we would live in Swansea, where my future husband had a lectureship.

In traditional fashion, the ceremony was to be held in the bride's country and that brought its own complications. The Catholic Church requires engaged couples to take part in a course of marriage preparation together. This is a sensible arrangement, which is greatly facilitated by the couple being in the same place or at least in the same country! In our case we managed to fit in the (then) minimum requirement of three meetings with a priest while my fiancé spent a short holiday with my family – and we were fortunate enough to find a priest with a good command of English. It was only much later that I discovered how much of a strain these sessions had been for my husband. The priest was as helpful as he could have been, but, nevertheless, my husband felt that he was only being accepted as a marriage partner for me 'on sufferance'.

At the time of our marriage, the Catholic Church still required the non-Catholic partner to promise that any children would be brought up as Catholics. The non-Catholic was also required to make it clear that the Catholic would be free to practise his or her religion. For us there was no problem on either count. I could not have gone into a marriage without being able to share what was most precious in my life with any children we might have and my fiancé had agreed to this. As for my practising my religion, we had taken that for granted. He therefore found the way in which the Church insisted on making sure that he was not a 'danger' to my faith or that of any children very hurtful: 'Why do they assume bad faith on my part? Why do they seem to think that I intend to do all sorts of things that I have no intention of doing?'

Although the Church's attitude to marrying non-Catholics has changed over the years, my husband still feels that some of the old suspiciousness, or at any rate over-protectiveness, lingers, as will become apparent later. His impression of the Catholic Church at the time was one of a Church doing all it could to keep its members in, to 'protect them from the world', its only interest in those outside being as potential converts. This, I am sure, is overstating the case, but the message from the Church, *as heard by my husband* at the time, could have been summed up as 'Thou shalt not.' Nor did the way I lived my faith at the time do much to dispel this misconception. Even so, I think he must have sensed that there was more to the Church than that. I do not imagine that he could have shown so much respect for something that could simply be reduced to a set of rules.

The human face of the Church at another level

While I was considering our marriage arrangements in a way which more or less followed the rule book, I was also aware of and touched by another, more profound, level of Catholicism. This concerned itself with meeting Christ in the Scriptures and in the life of the Church and with living the faith as a loving relationship with God and neighbour.

I remember discussing with a priest the question of the religious upbringing of any children the marriage may produce. Feeling quite pleased with myself, I advanced the argument that, if we did not agree to bring up the children as Catholics, our marriage would not be valid. In terms of Church rules, that was true, but the priest just looked at me as if I had completely missed the point – as indeed I had.

It was the same priest who commented, when he saw a photograph of my fiancé, 'He looks a really good man.' It is only now that the full implications of this comment are beginning to dawn on me: at one level I obviously knew that there were good people outside the Church, but I had not really considered the fact that God is the source of all goodness and that therefore all who are working for good and trying to lead good lives are on the same side, whether they are Church members or not. Thinking more deeply about this was to have important consequences for the way I later came to see my marriage.

During our engagement such thoughts were very much in the future. The 'rules and regulations' model of the Church was the one which my husband experienced from the 'official' Church that he met and also, to a large extent, from me. It was a model I felt safe with at the time and one which my husband was quick to expose in all its limitations: 'I don't mind you going to church on Sunday, but don't you think it would be better to go because you want to, rather than because there is a rule about it?'

Wedding

I recently attended, as an observer, a Marriage Preparation Day organised by Catholic Marriage Care.[4] Much emphasis was placed on the wedding ceremony itself in some of the video material which was used. Clearly, for some couples, arranging the wedding is a potential source of tension and disagreement particularly, but not only, for those where one partner is not a Catholic.

For ourselves, the question of where to get married never arose. I think we both took it for granted that, since I was a Catholic and my husband did not have any church connections, we would get married in a Catholic church and I think he accepted that we would go through whatever ceremony was the custom in the Catholic Church in Denmark at the time.

Since, for my husband, we were to be married in an unfamiliar church and in a foreign country, I thought it was important that the ceremony itself should be as comfortable and intelligible as possible. The wedding service was therefore conducted in English and we did not have a nuptial mass. I thought this would emphasise what divided rather than what united us, since we would not be able to receive communion together.

The wedding was important, but I think that, at the time, I was focusing more on our future life together. For me, and I am sure for my husband too, our marriage was an act of trust, taking one step at a time, on a shared path.

'Rite of passage'

When our daughter was born, after some years of marriage, the time had come for my husband to begin to live out his promise to have her brought up in the Catholic faith.

I am sure that her baptism was an occasion for him to think, again, about the promise he had made to me earlier that he would never come between me and the Church. He bought another cross, this time for our daughter, and gave it to her when she was baptised.

He has never commented on what he felt at attending her baptism – except for making it clear at the time that he did not want the public display involved in the usual Catholic practice of having a baptism during the Sunday mass. Such a wish is reasonable, I think, and we had a small, private celebration.

Thoughts about baptism

Baptism entails becoming a member of a church community. In the

Roman Catholic Church it always involves a renewal of baptismal vows by those present and it is therefore one of those occasions which emphasises the 'not-belonging' of those who are not part of the Church. My husband remained silent during the renewal of those vows – as was his right. He had done what he could by consenting to our daughter being baptised and by being present at the ceremony. In a sense it was, for him, a renewal of his promise to have any children we might have brought up in the Catholic faith.

A baptism, though fundamentally an occasion for joy, is bound to be difficult and painful in these circumstances. For the Roman Catholic parent it emphasises the fact that only part of the family belongs to the Church community, but for the non-believing parent it means, in a sense, handing over the child to an incomprehensible future in the hands of an incomprehensible organisation. It is an act of considerable trust (as had been our wedding). Tactful, sensitive baptismal preparation for the parents should (and I am sure in many cases does) lead to greater understanding on the part of the non-believer – and to an easing of the pain for both parents. A priest who has come to belief in God in adult life could have a particular gift in ministering to such couples.

As it was, I do not think the brief preparation we received added anything to my husband's understanding of what went on. But neither do I think anything I had to say helped him at all on this difficult occasion. Yet he did contribute to the liturgy: the cross he had bought our daughter was a sign of his commitment to have her brought up in the Church. There were to be times when this would entail his coming to church with her and with me.

The liturgy observed

My husband's parents had been occasional Anglican churchgoers and had sent him to Sunday School as a child. This experience had not led to belief for him and because of that he refused to be confirmed. I think this was an act of honesty and truthfulness rather than youthful rebellion. So when he began to go to church with me from time to time, he came as someone who had never believed in God though with some familiarity with a Christian church. His constant complaint was, and is, that there is no way of proving the reality which liturgical actions, Scripture and religious vocabulary point to. I have to agree with him. It is not possible to discover God in the same way as one can, for instance, discover the structure of a molecule or, to oversimplify, point to an object in a room. I remember once being asked by our daughter, when looking round a church, 'Where is God ?' As I could not point to a person, she said. 'God isn't.' I see what she meant and I think this is rather what my husband feels.

Impressions of the Church

There is a certain irony in that, having begun my working life in linguistic research I have now become involved, almost full time, in adult religious education work. Hence my husband's opportunities to observe Catholicism have grown more than he might have bargained for, when we got married. Over the years, far from losing interest, he has grown increasingly concerned that the Church should make use of language, visual presentation and religious art in a way that can convey its message to people today.

I once took part in a religious discussion programme on the radio, while my husband listened at home. When I got back, he said, 'Did it have to be so boring? I did not understand the introductory talk and during the discussion it was as if you were all in a different world – and not one that I felt at all attracted to.'

Christianity, like any other subject, has its technical language, its 'jargon', but unlike other subjects it does not see itself as a subject among others, but as a way of life. Theology can, of course, be studied as an academic subject, but the message of the Church is aimed at everyone and addresses the whole person, not just the intellect. The Gospels, on which the Church bases its teaching, invite a fundamental choice about how to live and who to entrust one's life to. They invite a commitment, in faith, which is not capable of scientific proof. In an age which is oriented towards science, this is a special difficulty, both for the Church, trying to convey its message, and for those outside who are trying to understand the words it uses.

The Church is sometimes accused of using archaic language, but that is not the fundamental difficulty. It is certainly not my husband's difficulty. The basic problem is the fact that the words point to a reality which, while not excluding reason, goes beyond it. To some extent religious language is bound to be 'words that mean nothing', for someone who has not experienced this reality. This difficulty seems to me to highlight the fact that Christianity is not, fundamentally, about the use of words, but about a way of life, an attitude to people and to the world around us.

While religious language does not speak to my husband, he is keenly aware of how the Church puts across her message in other ways, for instance through presentation and religious art.

Appearances are not all, but they are the first thing you see – of anything. Presentation, good or bad, is a language in itself. When an official Church publication changed its format, we looked at its vastly improved, new appearance and my husband said, 'This is really good!' It seemed to me that the message carried by good formatting is not only: 'This is well produced,' but also: 'We know that attention to detail, good layout and the use of modern technology are skills worth learning.'

Such a message of good presentation can reach out to those who are outside the Church in a way that has a chance of being understood – as our shared appreciation of the care and attention (dare I say, love?) spent on the production of this Church publication showed.

Religious art

My future husband had shown me in an art book a reproduction of 'Gelmeroda IX', a painting by Lyonel Feininger.[5] We both liked it and were determined to get a copy for our home. Shortly before we were married, we happened to walk into an art gallery in Copenhagen and learnt that a museum in Essen made copies of paintings from time to time. So we arranged for a copy of the Feininger to be sent to us.

The painting now sits above the fire in our sitting room. Although not an abstract, it is a highly stylised image; the German village of Gelmeroda is dominated by the church, the elegant steeple of which takes the viewer's glance upwards towards a small sphere poised at the very top of the steeple itself. The colours are mainly muted blues and greys, but there are some exciting rainbow tints too. Looking at it still gives us joy.

In a similar way, both of us were impressed by a simple modern church — built in traditional Austrian Tyrolean shape — we came across when we were on holiday near Innsbruck. It had clean lines and the light streamed in through a large stained-glass window. Good religious art and church architecture, for me, carry a message which can reach out where words fail.

It is my husband's appreciation of the beautiful (and not only the modern beautiful) which has led him to ask, again and again, 'Why does the Church seem to condone religious kitsch, such as luminous statues and the like? What kind of a message does that carry for the Church?'

He says this with an urgency which I know is prompted by his love for me and for what is important to me.

When the new *Catechism of the Catholic Church* was published in 1994, I was heartened to see religious art discussed in the chapter on the commandment 'Not to bear false witness'. The emphasis is on the positive rather than the negative: that is, on the importance of truthfulness.

About sacred art it says:

> Truth is beautiful in itself. Truth in words, the rational expression of the knowledge of . . . reality is necessary to man, who is endowed with intellect. But truth can also find complementary forms of human expression, above all when it is a matter of evoking what is beyond words: the depths of the human heart,

the exaltations of the soul, the mystery of God . . . Genuine
sacred art draws man to adoration, to prayer and to the love of
God . . . [6]

The sensibilities of others

Religious art, good or bad, may be the first thing someone notices
on entering a church building but, for a non-Catholic spouse, the
parish newsletter is often the 'immediate face' of the Catholic
Church. Attention to wording, especially as regards relations
between Catholics and non-Catholics is therefore particularly
important. 'Assume good intentions from other people!' my husband once said to me, in a completely different context. Wording
can sometimes so obscure good intentions that they are no longer
apparent to the casual observer.

The Catholic Church most often touches non-Catholics when
they wish to marry Catholics. In the diocese where I live marriage
regulations now require couples to give six months' notice of their
intention to marry. It is at these times that a most sensitive hand is
needed and we are all growing all the time, priests as well as lay
people. On one occasion, when the parish newsletter carried a
reminder about the marriage regulations, my husband was very
upset, because of the long list of actions which were mentioned as
'forbidden' in connection with a 'mixed' marriage. The newsletter
entry seemed to work on the assumption that, unless strongly
warned, people would be likely to take those actions. It is not often
I see my husband upset, but on this occasion it took me some time
to discover that it was not the regulations he objected to, but the
lack of consideration for people, which the phrasing of the entry
seemed to imply. 'Non-Catholics have thoughts, views and feel-
ings,' he said. 'Why can't the Church assume that, at least, we *might*
have good intentions?' It was then he mentioned how, when we
were preparing to get married, he had felt treated as a potential
danger to my faith.

My husband knows, of course, that newsletters are often written against the clock and in such circumstances it is easy to put bluntly what, ideally, should have been delicately phrased. But his plea that the non-Catholic spouse should be (and, I am sure, often is) treated with consideration, deserves attention. A newsletter can be a kind of 'window on the Church'. It is important that the view through the window is inviting.

Getting through

Non-believers are not the only people looking at the Church and drawing conclusions about it. Sometimes, people look at the Church because they want to come into full membership with it. On occasion I have been asked to have private talks with people who had approached my parish about becoming Catholics. Not so long ago I had arranged to see a couple who wanted to discuss the Church in some detail, before being received. 'What's it like living as Catholic?' they asked. 'What's it like going to confession and what does the Church say about re-marriage?' Those were only some of the questions they brought up; what they wanted from me was a share of my experience. Quoting from a rule book, as I had very largely done before my marriage and during the early part of it, would have meant badly short-changing these deeply thinking people. So I told them how I was trying to live my faith, about how I prayed, how I used the sacrament of reconciliation or 'confession' in the context of spiritual development, and about how I saw my marriage as a vocation and a life-long commitment. We did talk about 'rules', but the emphasis was on relating to God, to other people and to ourselves.

These conversations brought my own life under review. I realised that relationships, with God in prayer and with other people in friendship, are now at the centre of my life as a Christian and a Roman Catholic. Rules of behaviour are there to support my life as a Catholic within the Church community, but they are not an aim in themselves. These sessions with the couple left me tired but happy, because I knew that I had given of myself rather than quoted 'chapter and verse'. When I told my husband, he seemed to understand instinctively that these conversations were quite different to those we had had in preparation for our own marriage. The practise of the Catholic faith that he now saw in me was of a deeper and more personal kind than it had been earlier. His response was different too. I was able to share some of the flavour of the sessions with him and he understood why they were important to me. Through his university teaching he, too, knows about getting through to people.

Loving regard

My husband has been faithful to the promises he made at the beginning of our marriage – never to come between me and the Church and to give any children we might have the chance to grow up as Catholics. He has walked with me, observing this Church which he does not belong to but which, because of me, affects his life so profoundly, with eyes ever open to the signals it sends out. From his reactions I know that above all he looks for truthfulness and authenticity: for me to be true to what I believe and for the Church to proclaim its message in a way that is worthy of the content.

His observation has not led to faith for him, but it has led him to what I can only describe as a kind of 'loving regard' for the Church and its affairs. In the many penetrating comments he has made about the Church over the years, he has always looked for what is best in the Church and seen, very clearly, what could be better. I could say that he has been holding up a mirror to the Church and also to the way I live my faith. The occasions when I have been forced to take stock of my attitudes and assess what is essential in my faith and what is a frill, or a sin, have been times for growth both in our relationship and in my relationship with God and the Church.

In this way, far from being a danger to my faith, his looking at the Church and what I believe, from the outside, and telling me what he sees, has strengthened and developed my faith, and has been an invitation to a continued dialogue with him about matters of belief. An, originally, non-Catholic friend who married a Catholic once put it to me, 'By the time we'd been married a few years, my husband was a very different kind of Catholic!' After more than twenty years of marriage I know that I, too, am a very different kind of Catholic.

Summary

FOR NON-BELIEVERS

For people who do not believe in God, it is easy to think of themselves as having no role to play in the religious practice of their marriage partners, other than the passive one of permitting that practice and being open to the possibility of any children being brought up in the Church.

In reality, non-believers can have a positive role to play by the way they observe and comment on the religious practice of their spouses, on the local church community and on the 'official' face of the Church as seen in publications, presentation and art. It is important that non-believing spouses say what they think, not only for their own integrity but also for the religious development of the believers they are married to – and for the self-understanding of the Church. It may be a contribution that only non-believers can make.

FOR BELIEVERS

Marrying a non-believer may, at first, appear mainly as a 'problem' for Catholics (or other believers). But, especially for believers brought up in a legalistic form of religion such a 'mixed marriage' can produce a deepening understanding of their faith, leading to a way of life prompted by love of God, of other people (and of self). Such an attitude also implies a profound respect for those who, in truth, cannot say that they believe in God, but whose honest questioning is their contribution to the religious dimension of their marriages.

FOR CLERGY

The emphasis on rules has lessened in the Catholic Church, but it is still the face of the Church that is seen by many non-Catholics (and Catholics too). In marriage (and baptismal) preparation it is important to put rules in their human context and always to work on the initial assumption that 'both halves' of a couple come in good faith and with good will.

In many cases the way to understanding religion, especially for a non-believer, may not, in the first instance, be through religious (for example, liturgical) language, but rather through the 'signals' sent out by the newsletter, by religious publications, and by religious art.

CHAPTER THREE

Across the Boundaries

The incarnation of gospel values in a modernized culture, can only be done by a mature, faith-filled, educated Christian laity.

Peter Schiveller, SJ[1]

Don't be ashamed to practise the ordinary, necessary actions that bring us to the love of God.

St Francis de Sales[2]

When I was thinking of getting married, a friend said to me, 'Have you considered the whole business of going to church alone?' This friend was not trying to prevent me, merely to make sure that I had faced all the issues before committing myself. I had indeed considered the issues, as far as it is possible to do so in advance, and the answer to the question was, and is, that I felt called to this marriage in spite of the difficulties implied in marrying a non-believer. (That was not to say that I was not in love and loved him (!), but with this love went a strong sense of vocation.)

The Christian in society: then and now

I had good reason to think carefully before embarking on marriage.

In today's society, in the developed world, all Christians, to some extent, live in religious isolation. In addition, Christians married to non-believers, inevitably, face some religious isolation at home. They live in a double isolation, however much their marriage partners try to understand and listen to them. This has not always been so.

I am writing this chapter during Lent and my Lent book this year is St Bernard of Clairvaux's twelfth-century treatise, *On the Love of God*.[3] Reading St Bernard, I am struck by his references to 'non-believers' always meaning 'non-Christians', not 'people who do not believe in God'. On the contrary, Bernard makes it clear that these people, precisely because they believe in God, have certain obligations towards Him who made them.

This is not the place, nor am I qualified, to trace the history of 'non-belief', but I would like to give a few examples that I have come across. These illustrate some 'tacit assumptions', in religious matters, from centuries closer to our own time than that of St Bernard.

In her book on religious dissenters (for example, Quakers and Congregationalists) in sixteenth- and seventeenth-century rural England, Margaret Spufford has painted a vivid picture of a world very different from ours. In this world were isolated instances of 'non–belief', in the sense of not believing in God, but the general pattern of religious awareness was one of familiarity with and interest in religious topics. In the lives of ordinary people in the seventeenth century there was

> . . . a kind of general familiarity, in the alehouse, the cobbler's shop, the miller's, the baker's, and many cottages, even of those exempt from taxation on grounds of poverty, with religious discussion and arguments, which no longer exists in contemporary society.[4]

Owen Chadwick speaks of atheism as a fashion among an aristocratic elite in France during the late sixteenth- and seventeenth-centuries. However, they still valued Christian belief in those they wished to trust!

In a revealing passage, Chadwick quotes Voltaire:

> I want my lawyer, tailor, valets, even my wife, to believe in God; I think that if they do I shall be robbed less and cheated less.[5]

In the nineteenth century, on the other hand, the 'daring' fashion of the few had become a more widespread attitude of 'non-belief' or at any rate detachment of religion from culture.[6]

In our own time, Cardinal Ratzinger has spoken of modern Europe as the place where a concept of culture which was distinct from, or even opposed to religion first appeared.[7] To many people now religion appears a quaint relic from earlier times. A few years ago, the preacher Brian Hebblethwaite said that one of the things that had frightened him in the last few decades was the fact that more and more young people came up to university with no religious background whatsoever.

> Religious people may seem to them like quaint survivors, rather like the changing of the guard, or beefeaters.[8]

According to another contemporary writer, Godfried Daneels, religion, where it does exist, is increasingly being relegated to the private sphere and Europe has become a continent where God is more and more absent from public life. Religion is pushed aside to the private sphere and is ignored by a kind of 'practical atheism', which is indifferent to the fundamental questions of life.[9] Similar trends can be observed elsewhere; for instance, in the United States and Australia.[10]

This is the society in which I, and other practising Christians, try to live our faith. Fr Columba Cary–Elwes compares the situation of Christians today with the times of St Benedict in the sixth century, saying that, in our time, we once again live in 'a non-believing or half-believing world.'[11]

It is impossible for Christians, especially those in marriages with people who do not believe in God, not to be affected by this separation of religion and culture, and indeed the demise of religion from the consciousness of many people.

For example, in the *Directory on Mixed Marriages for the Catholic Church in England and Wales*, a parallel is drawn between marriage in which one partner is a Roman Catholic and the other is unbaptised and a marriage where one partner, though baptised, has no real experience of Christian faith or practice. The *Directory* takes the view that, in both these cases, it is wise to assume that the Christian view of marriage may well be entirely unfamiliar.[12]

Outward signs of faith

The teachings of Christianity may well be unfamiliar to a large number of people now, but the Christian faith has left its mark on the landscape, certainly in some parts of Europe, and I am not thinking of the established Churches only.

Holidaying in the French Alps (our first holiday alone together after our daughter had left to go to university), we stayed in a small village near Chamonix. On our first afternoon, we went for a stroll and came upon a large, wooden, wayside cross. To me it was not a great surprise to see this simple cross. France is, after all (in tradition at least) a Catholic country. But my husband commented on it and throughout this holiday in the Haute-Savoie we noticed wayside crosses in many other places. (In fact there was one directly opposite the hotel where we stayed.)

The crosses were usually simple, and lovingly kept, often with flowers planted at the foot of the Cross or placed in pots around it. These outward signs of Christianity and of a living Christian faith were a great comfort to me and made me realise just how devoid of such signs was my everyday existence in the UK.

Wayside crosses belong mainly, I think, within the Roman Catholic tradition. They might not be acceptable or helpful to those of other Christian traditions, but my reaction to these particular crosses showed me how far we have gone in the UK (and many other Western countries) towards viewing religion as a purely private matter. There are churches, yes, but the 'small-scale', more personal, signs, for instance on a street corner, or in a room, are largely missing.

I am, obviously, not under the illusion that all of France is devoutly Catholic (or Christian). Nevertheless, in the rural setting of the Haute-Savoie the outward signs of Christian belief were still visible, and cared for, and they gave me strength.

Seeing the wayside crosses and reacting to them made me look with fresh eyes at the 'outward' signs of Christianity in our house, when we got home. For example, there is the crucifix above our bed which was a wedding present. I now realise that I must look at it often, because I have noticed that when I am away, I tend to turn my eyes to the spot where it would have been – and see a blank wall!

Some years ago, my husband went to a conference in Czechoslovakia. Then, it was still one nation and under communist rule. The conference was held in the Tatra mountains and my husband brought back from there an embroidered picture, which we have since had framed and put up in our dining room. It is a celebration scene: men drinking, women carrying flowers and presents, and in the centre of the picture a table with bread and wine. To the right of the table some women are admiring a baby, to the left there is a church. It is a colourful, naive picture. It is also a statement of faith: the presents are obviously for a baby who has just been baptised, perhaps in the church we see in the picture. The bread and wine on the table could be seen as food and drink for the celebration, but since only bread and wine are shown, they are also a reminder of the Eucharist: baptism, Eucharist, the Church. I sometimes wonder who embroidered that picture and how it came to be sold in a country where Christians were still being persecuted. I thought it would be a good picture for our dining room and a priest friend came to bless it before we put it up. 'May all who eat here be blessed,' he said. When I look at the picture his words often come back to me.

As I sit at my desk writing, the icon of Christ, a Christmas present from my daughter, is before me. Until I came to write this chapter, I had not realised how much religious art matters to me as a support for my faith, nor was I aware that some of the pieces in our house mark stages along our way as a family. I am grateful that my husband is happy to have these waymarks in our house. A cross or a religious picture which speaks to me can prompt and sustain religious actions. Even an 'accidental cross' can be a help in daily life and especially in times of need. Sheila Cassidy, the British doctor who was imprisoned in Chile for helping a human rights campaigner, speaks of the support she got from 'finding' a simple cross in the metal bands of the bunk above her own.

> I lay on my bunk and looked at the metal bands of the mesh which supported the mattress of the upper tier. I had long ago learned to look for the sign of the cross in doors and windows and all things square, for it reminded me of Christ and helped me to focus my attention on Him and pray in unlikely places such as the bus or the hospital. At the Posta [where she worked in Chile] there had been a long corridor with a door at the end and I used to walk slowly down the passage with its yellowed tiles and look up towards the 'cross' as if I were walking down the aisle of a church.[13]

Later in the book she speaks of her need for a crucifix. Although not usually a devotee of religious objects d'art, the crucifix reminded her of God when circumstances in prison got a little easier and she feared she might forget her need for Him.[14]

In a largely non-religious environment this kind of visual support, whether intended as Christian symbols or not, can be a help to a Christian. In the home of a family of believers I imagine that a cross or an icon can be not only a sign of the presence of God but a prompter to prayer for the whole family – perhaps sometimes for prayer together.

For the believing member(s) of a family where not all are Christians, such images can still be silent reminders of God, prompters to brief prayer, or cries for help in the many different, and sometimes difficult, situations of family life. Such images are also witnesses to the faith of those who believe and sometimes silent witnessing is all that is called for.

On the other hand, speaking of God and of religious issues in everyday life is also a way of acknowledging the presence of God. In a family where only one parent believes, the question of when to put such issues into words requires especially careful thought.

'The fullness of fidelity'

St Francis de Sales, writing to the wife of a (perhaps less than committed) Roman Catholic who was irritated by her wish to spend time in prayer, asked her whether she had been over-eager and bustling in her religious practise and perhaps neglected her household.[15] In other words, had she put her family off by talking about religion morning, noon and night and not really being available for what was not explicitly religious activity?

I can remember a stage in the earlier part of my married life, when I seemed to 'edit out' conversation about non-religious matters as being less important. For the committed Christian family member there is a danger, not only of 'over-eagerness', but also of not being sufficiently interested in all aspects of family life. On 'perseverance' in family life, Dolores Lecky wrote:

> *Physical presence alone does not constitute the fullness of fidelity.* Emotional and spiritual presence, full and honest participation in the daily rounds of family ritual are necessary if one is truly to persevere. It is not enough merely to be looking on. To persevere in family life one must face the reality of all that is there, from caring for children to sickness to rejection to death. All constitute life in community.[16]

My husband says I have a one-track mind, which means, on the positive side, that I am quite good at concentrating on things I am interested in; the negative side is that I tend to shut out what I care less about. As I work in a Church context and often find this absorbing, I have to be particularly careful to switch to other tracks as well. On the other hand, never talking about religion also has its consequences, for all the members of the family. There is clearly a balance to be struck.

Faith without words

Not so long after we were married I came across a passage from the First Letter of St Peter. It must have impressed me because I underlined it in my Bible. Peter reminds the early Christians that husbands who do not believe are sometimes better won over simply by the way their wives behave, '*without a word spoken*'.[17]

This attitude seems to be the one advocated by Charles de Foucauld for his order of 'Little Brothers and Sisters of Jesus', whose members go out to work among the poorest of the poor. Charles wanted his followers to preach only by their silence, which, he said, was 'always more eloquent than words'.[18]

'Silent witnessing' can undoubtedly speak powerfully, but I think believers need some opportunity to speak about their faith, both at home and elsewhere. What I suspect the First Letter of St Peter and the instructions of Charles de Foucauld have in mind is that actions speak louder than words. This is not to dismiss words altogether, but to say that without actions words are certainly of no use.[19]

When our daughter was about seven, she gave me an American coin, saying that she thought I would like it, because it had the words 'In God we trust' stamped on it. I cannot remember ever telling her that I trusted God, or asking her to do the same, but she must have picked it up, somehow. As a friend put it to me, 'Children are quite good at "sussing out" what is important to you, even if you have not always put it into words.'

Speaking of what I believe

On the other hand there must be a danger in never speaking out about what I believe. Fr Columba Cary–Elwes has something to say about the dangers to faith which are characteristic of our time. In his comments on the section of the Benedictine Rule which deals with the reception of guests, of whatever religious persuasion, he draws the following parallel with family life:

> St Benedict makes a special point about the faith of the guest. Today we are once again embedded in a non-believing or half-believing world. In our homes we should distinguish, receive all as Christ, yes, because He is there, but often in the 'chains' of unbelief. We may think we are strong, yet, if all mention of faith, which we hold dear, has to be avoided – I am thinking of habitual guests – then things of the faith fall into the background, then become taboo in our subconscious mechanism of choice. We stunt our faith, and, given some great moral shock, one morning we find our faith is dead. With real open friendship in which differences are eagerly discussed, such encounters can stimulate our faith.[20]

'Real open friendship' must surely exist between husband and wife, if a marriage is to have a chance and that includes being able to tell the other that it is hard not to share faith in God.[21]

I am sure that different situations call for different approaches. However, I think it is not for nothing that people who, in an Evangelical Christian context, have decided to 'opt for Christ' are asked to tell another person of their decision. There is a sense in which something I have spoken about becomes more real to me, and more of a commitment, even if the other person does not really understand what I am talking about.

The isolation in which Christians often live in today's society and also in many families makes it all the more necessary for them to seek the support of other Christians. They need interaction with other Christians to talk about their faith and also to be part of a worshipping community.

I once helped organise a small group of young mothers who met at our church. The group was originally set up for mothers to talk about the religious upbringing of their children, to share ideas and so on. However, I am sure that the main reason why some of the mothers came was to have a chance to talk to like-minded people about their faith. As it turned out, many of them had few people they could talk to about their faith and, by implication, about what they were trying to pass on to their children. Some of the mothers who turned up were married to non-believers and some were married to Christians of other denominations. The group has now been wound up, but what kept a number of those mothers coming back year after year was, I think, the chance to talk to other adults about their faith, in an informal and welcoming environment.

Church groups where adults meet to talk about their faith, or to learn more about it, can also take on an important function as a support structure for people who cannot share their faith at home.

I remember at a retreat I attended, a woman made precisely this point. The group were discussing the isolation of Christians in society and she said that, in some cases, Christians were far more isolated at home if their husbands or wives or children did not believe. Another lady said, quite simply, 'There is no one I can share my faith with.' By 'no one' she meant no one in her family or among her friends. So, the retreat was a rare chance for her to be able to talk to someone else, at some length, about her faith.

Visiting preacher

At a Sunday mass I attended recently, the visiting preacher brought out particularly powerfully the difficulty for Christians in marriages with non-believers, or whose children have become non-believers. He spoke about the early Christians bearing witness and how people nowadays were rarely called on to die for their faith. He went on to the much more common difficulty of speaking lovingly about one's faith in a family where not all members believe. Somehow, he visualised for the congregation the pain and difficulty Christians feel in this situation, stressing that the non-believer must also be respected and that there were no easy solutions. I cannot remember his exact words, but his sermon opened up an area which was evidently of deep concern to many.

After mass I could see the impression he had made. Someone sitting next to me started a long conversation about living the faith in a marriage with a non-believer and trying to hand it on to the children and, as I left the church, I noticed that someone else was in tears and being comforted. When things are hard to bear, it can be liberating to talk about them, even to cry about them, with someone who understands. What this preacher had done was to create the opportunity for people to open up to each other in a way that made such sharing possible.

Christian isolation — or secular neutrality?

The support of the wider Christian community is always important for a Christian and especially now that Western society is largely post-Christian. However, I think there is a danger of Christians turning in on themselves in their sense of isolation, feeling that they can only talk about God with fellow-Christians; that, indeed, the only people they can really talk to are fellow-Christians. Before they know where they are, such people may find themselves mixing only with other Christians and going out only to 'Christian' events. In effect, they are hiding in a ghetto.

From seeking the support of other Christians, which is in itself a worthy aim, some people can, perhaps without realising it, slide into an attitude of excluding all non-Christians from their lives. This may appear an easy option, seemingly avoiding the tension of living in a post-Christian world but this attitude carries with it the danger of forgetting that God loves the whole of creation. It is this creation He sent His Son to save and that He has called Christians to go into the world to make disciples of all the nations.[22] In a ghetto the call to mission is easily forgotten.

Christianity 'bowdlerised'

Choosing to live in a 'ghetto' as a reaction to 'the world' is one extreme. The other is to excise all reference to one's beliefs from everyday conversation, except when talking to other believers – so that all mention of God or religion is, so to speak, 'bowdlerised' from one's conversation. This, too, is dangerous and can lead to a kind of split life where one behaves in one way with Christians and in a completely different way with non-believers. Even bearing in mind that there is 'a time and place' for everything, never being able to talk about one's religious beliefs, however fleetingly, can mean never really being able to be oneself. I can still remember my surprise (and pleasure!) when an American mother whose son attended the same playgroup as my daughter spoke quite openly of church groups that she belonged to. I had been used to being far more reserved about such matters. And Sheila Cassidy wrote of her inability to tell her cell mates that she marked the 'cross' on the bunk above hers with black wool, so that others would be able to see it too. When she was making the cross, she said that she was just playing, but, later on, when she was forced to speak about her religion and her vocation to be a nun, she was surprised to find that her cell mates, who did not believe in God, understood her concept of commitment much better than the average Christian might have done. As Sheila came to understand, these girls, too, had given themselves without reserve.[23]

'Coming out'

'Coming out' as a Christian, even in less challenging circumstances than those experienced by Sheila Cassidy, can be a great relief, as well as an act of honesty.

We had let our neighbours park their car on our drive overnight but I had to tell them that I needed to get our car out early on Sunday morning. What I had not told them was that I needed the car to go to Church. It was our neighbour who said, 'Of course, I know you go to church on Sunday morning.' I thought: 'My editing mechanism needs reviewing!' Owning up to being a Christian, (even though the 'owning up' had been done for me in this instance) was a great relief. A friend of mine, who makes no secret of her Christian belief, found it made for greater honesty all round at her workplace now that she talked openly about the Christian side of her life. It also means that she is asked awkward questions, particularly where ethical matters are concerned.

Not mentioning my religious beliefs is sometimes due to, quite legitimate, fears that I may appear to be trying to force religion on to another person. Religious beliefs can appear as a threat to those who do not share them. In a message for World Mission Day, Pope John Paul II invited those called to mission to show non-believers 'signs of love' so as to overcome their disbelief and their fears.[24]

Neither to be locked, fearfully, in a ghetto looking only to the past nor inspiring fear of the unknown in the non-believers around me but rather showing 'signs of love' for everyone I meet, this is the challenge I see for myself. And so it is for all Christians in a non-believing world and never more so than in a marriage with a non-believer. The way I live my faith must be authentic and must also take into account the attitudes of my family and others around me.

During our marriage preparation I said (with regard to children, but it is equally true of my husband): 'How could I *not* wish to share what is most precious in my life, my faith, with those closest to me?'

I think this wish to share is at the heart of Christ's command to go and 'make disciples': it is in the nature of love to wish to share itself. But it is also in the nature of love to respect the other person's point of view, to be aware 'where he or she is at' and to be ready to wait for the right time for talking about matters of faith, or certain aspects of faith. The loneliness of waiting for the right moment can be hard to bear, but forcing oneself on the other person would mean 'loving' oneself more that the other. A priest put this to me very graphically: 'God does not rape anyone.'

Our daughter once asked me, 'Is it not difficult when you are a Catholic and Dad does not believe in God? I mean, it is something pretty basic to disagree about!' In a sense, she was echoing my friend's question all those years ago. ('Have you considered the whole business of going to church alone?')

Yes, it is difficult, at times very difficult, but I have found that this very difficulty has drawn my husband and me together, not least because of his respect for what I believe and his willingness to talk about religious matters. I have also come to realise that Christ is at work in him too and that the goodness I see in him is not different to the goodness of Christians. Both have their root in Christ, though my husband would not see it like that. This very goodness provides a basis for sharing across the boundary between us. It has also inspired me to investigate further why Christ seems to be so clearly at work in non-believers such as my husband.

Summary

FOR NON-BELIEVERS

In Western society many people now do not believe in God. This is a new cultural phenomenon. Many Christians therefore feel isolated in what is largely a post-Christian environment. Since faith in God is at the centre of the life of committed Christians, it is doubly painful for them not to be able to share it with a spouse. On the other hand, respect for the other person's point of view demands that there should never be coercion, only a wish for ever greater openness and that includes sharing the pain of religious isolation.

FOR BELIEVERS

In Western society Christian beliefs and practice are now valued less and less. It is especially important for a Christian married to a non-believer to value all areas of life and to know when to speak of religion and when to be silent and at the same time hold on to a Christian way of life. Crosses, icons and other religious images can support faith and children often pick up religious 'vibes' without many words being spoken. Two predominant temptations for Christians today are hiding in a 'ghetto' and stifling faith by never talking about it. Seeing Christ in all others can help Christians to cross the boundary between belief and non-belief and to meet (especially) a non-believing spouse in real open friendship.

FOR CLERGY

Marriages between Christians and non-Christians and between Christians and baptised non-believers have similar characteristics. From a religious viewpoint, Christians are likely, in both cases, to live in 'double isolation' (socially and in the marriage itself). Married life for such Christians requires much tact, so that practising the faith can be perceived by the other person not as a threat but as an (open) invitation. Support from the Christian community and preaching and teaching that speak to their situation can help Christians live such marriages in truth and love.

CHAPTER FOUR

'All That is Right'

Let us pray
for those who do not believe in God,
that they may find Him
by sincerely following all that is right.

Good Friday intercessions[1]

To be not only an anonymous Christian, but to know what
one is – this is grace.

Karl Rahner[2]

Good Friday prayers for the whole world

On Good Friday Roman Catholics, like many other Christians,
come together to remember the Lord's Passion. The account of
His trial, crucifixion and death for all mankind is read from the
Gospel of St John. In the Catholic Church this reading is followed
by a series of prayers for the whole world (known as the Good
Friday Intercessions), focusing on specific groups, one at a time.
The Church, in response to the sacrifice of the Lord, prays for all
those He died for, beginning with the Church itself: 'Let us pray for

the holy Church of God throughout the world, . . . ' Prayers follow for the Pope, the other bishops, for priests and deacons, for those with a specific ministry in the Church (for instance readers) and all members of the Church.

The focus then turns to people on the 'threshold' of the Church, that is, those preparing for baptism. The Intercessions move on to other Christian Churches, praying for the unity of all Christians and the Jewish people are prayed for as 'the first to hear the word of God'. The attention of the prayers is then directed to all those individuals or members of religious groups who do not believe in Christ but who 'walk before God in sincerity of heart.'

Almost at the end of the Intercessions, and at the end of the prayers for people defined by the way they relate to God and the Church, comes the prayer for 'Those who do not believe in God. That they may find Him by sincerely following all that is right.'

Listening to the Intercessions, I am always reminded of con-centric circles. In the Roman Catholic Church, the Intercessions begin at the centre and gradually move outwards until they reach those at the very edge of the circle, furthest from the centre.[3] As the prayers progress, I feel that they reach out to all mankind, how-ever distant from the Church. I also feel the pain of having to pray for my husband among those furthest from the Church, those who *do not believe in God.*

The Catholic Church is not the only one to pray liturgically for those who do not believe in God. The Anglican Benedictine com-munity at West Malling in Kent have a beautiful petition 'For those who seek God but cannot yet name him . . . ', which is said daily as part of the Intercessions at the Eucharist.[4]

It seems to me that 'following all that is right' is also a way of 'seeking God', even if the search is not a conscious one.

For many people nowadays belief in God makes no sense at all. This is not necessarily because they lack good will but because the message of the Church, for whatever reason, does not make sense to them or seem relevant to their lives. Such people are often very 'Christian' in their behaviour. One of the eucharistic prayers of the mass speaks of the dead 'whose faith is known to you alone'. It seems a merciful interpretation of this prayer[5] to see it as including those who sought to do *all that is right* during their lifetime without ever coming to explicit faith in God.

Doing '*All that Is Right*'

Over the years I have become increasingly aware of the contrast between the distance of non-believers from the centre, as they appear in the Good Friday Intercessions, and the very 'Christian' behaviour I see in my husband. He is often the one who 'does' the Christian living, notices a student needing encouragement, finds time to check on the Internet those references I need to a German theologian he has never heard of and in a language he does not understand. By his behaviour my husband is often closer to the centre than I am.

'CHRISTIANS BY BEHAVIOUR'

My husband and people like him could, with good reason, be called 'Christians by behaviour'. This, of course does not make them official members of the Church, but it does establish a link between all people who are trying to do 'what is right', whether inside or outside the Church.

It is important for all Christians to be aware of this link, but, I think, especially for those married to non-believers. I know it stops me from becoming smug and too satisfied with myself and it helps me keep my eye on what really matters in life and by which we will all be judged.

SEPARATING THE SHEEP FROM THE GOATS

The passage in the Gospel of St Matthew which describes the Day of Judgement, when Christ appears before all peoples and separates the good from the bad (sheep from goats), is one of the best known in the Bible. It is clear from St Matthew's account that what will count is not whether someone knew Christ or had come to explicit belief in Him during their lifetime, but whether they acted according to the promptings of their conscience to love their neighbour.

> Lord, when did we see you hungry and feed you; thirsty and give you drink? . . . I tell you solemnly, in so far as you did this to the least of these brothers of mine, you did it to me.[6]

In this passage, there is no mention of explicit belief in Christ, but it is taken for granted that every human being can feel, and accept or reject, the promptings to act in a neighbourly way. The way they react to these promptings will judge them.

The call to neighbourly love is so important that the Vatican II document on the Church states that someone who is 'incorporated into the Church', but does not 'persevere in charity' is not saved.[7]

I have been familiar with this passage from Matthew for most of my life, but somehow it had not occurred to me to relate it to what I had seen in my husband and to link it with what I felt we could share in our marriage. I needed help from another quarter, before I could fully realise that.

Rahner and the Anonymous Christian

The first reference I ever heard to the German theologian Karl Rahner was in a joke about how someone had offered to 'translate' his works into German – meaning that his style was too convoluted even for Germans to understand! This was not an introduction likely to make me want to read Rahner, but the next time I heard about him was from a priest who recommended his works as being helpful for a spirituality of everyday Christian living. I think that was when I began to get interested. Shortly afterwards I picked up a secondhand book with a selection of his works, mainly on spirituality, and I began to realise both that Rahner had something important to say to me and that he was perfectly capable of writing in a 'non-convoluted' way. A set of short meditations for Holy Week that he had written for Bavarian Radio were my 'taster'. I found them helpful and I wanted to read more.

RAHNER AND NEIGHBOURLY LOVE

Love of neighbour is so important in Rahner's work that he states that whenever someone truly loves his neighbour, this love is also a love of God.

> Wherever a genuine love of man attains its proper nature and its moral absoluteness and depth, it is in addition always so underpinned and heightened by God's saving grace that it is also love of God, whether it be explicitly considered to be such a love by the person who loves or not.[8]

Further on in the same work Rahner says that,

> . . . it is radically true . . . that whoever does not love the brother whom he 'sees', also cannot love God whom he does not see, and that one can love God whom one does not see only by loving one's visible brother lovingly.[9]

Rahner himself practised what he preached. William Dych, a former student of Rahner's, told of how he would accompany the theologian on trips to the supermarket. Rahner would buy groceries, which they then took to some poor family who Rahner had met, perhaps years earlier, but whose need he had not forgotten.[10]

As I am married to somebody who 'loves his neighbour lovingly', I began to wonder about this very Christian behaviour in somebody who does not call himself a Christian.

The enforced immobility of a 'frozen' shoulder gave me the opportunity to read Rahner in greater detail. It was then that I first read his description of the man or woman who seeks to do all that is right but who has not come to belief in God or Christ. This person is Rahner's anonymous Christian. I remember reading one of his key passages on this concept just before I attended a conference where it was discussed as something new and exciting and very helpful for Christians today. Rahner describes the anonymous Christian in a number of different ways in different contexts, but he returns to the practise of neighbourly love as *the* mark of Christ on a person, whether that person knows Christ or not.

Key questions

In trying to live my marriage with a non-believer, two questions kept reappearing: 'How can I live a Christian Marriage with someone who does not believe in Christ – or God?'; and, 'How can I share my Christian faith with someone who does not believe?' (I am not thinking of mission, but of living and sharing with someone who does not believe.)

I already had a hint of an answer to the second question, because my husband often behaves in a more 'Christian' way than I do. I had no doubt that, in some areas at least, we were not only sharing Christian practice, but he was, through his example, leading me towards a better practice of my faith. And, pondering the first question, I thought further about Rahner's anonymous Christian.

THE ANONYMOUS CHRISTIAN

Rahner describes the anonymous Christian as someone who

> . . . prior to the explicitness of official ecclesiastical faith . . . undertakes and lives the duty of each day in the quiet sincerity of patience, in devotion to his material duties and the demands made upon him by the persons under his care.[11]

These words accurately and lovingly portray what I daily see in my husband. I was beginning to find a theology for what I had already observed in the person I am closest to.

THE 'SUPERNATURAL EXISTENTIAL': EYES TO SEE CHRIST WITH

The idea of the anonymous Christian presupposes that there is some ability, some sense, with which people can turn towards God, and Christ, even if they do not yet know Him. Rahner calls this the 'supernatural existential'.

> The believer will grasp that God's self-communication offered to all . . . constitutes the goal of all creation and – since God's word and will effect what they say – that, *even before he freely takes up an attitude to it, it stamps and determines man's nature and lends it a character which we may call a 'supernatural existential'*.[12]

Thus the 'stamp of Christ' is already on every human being and this 'stamp' is shared by an 'explicit' Christian and an 'implicit' or anonymous Christian. Both can be moved by and are potentially obedient to the grace which has its source in God. The difference between them is that the 'explicit' Christian knows and acknowledges the source of the grace to which he or she is responding.

As mentioned earlier, the possibility of serving Christ without knowing him is described graphically in the Gospel of St Matthew. ('In so far as you did this to the least of these brothers of mine, you did it to me.') Rahner explains:

> Christians have always been aware, at least in principle, that they can know, realise and prove to be credible their hoping and loving relationship to the incomprehensible mystery of their lives only in the unconditional love of their neighbour, in which alone they can really burst open the hell of their egoism . . . Where this love is truly at work, the spirit of Jesus is there, even when He is not named, as Matthew 25 clearly teaches us.[13]

Rahner's reflections on the way in which all human beings can accept grace, even without coming to explicit belief, came as a great comfort to me. They made it clear that Christians and non-believers do not, after all, live in separate compartments but are able to share, to some extent at least, the religious aspects of life.

SHARING MARRIED LIFE AND FAITH WITH A NON-BELIEVER

The concept of anonymous Christianity added another dimension to the way I saw my marriage. It made me think that with every neighbourly act we did, we were following Christ and hence at least beginning to live a Christian marriage. Thus loving our neighbour lovingly *together* was beginning to appear to me to be the way in which I, as Christian, could live a Christian marriage with a non-believer, while still respecting my husband's integrity as an 'honest non-believer'. The knowledge that I was (and am) sharing some of my most deeply held religious convictions with my husband and am able to talk to him about them showed me that there was a way in which I could share my faith with him.

After finding answers to my two key questions which satisfied me, it would have been easy to stop and think, 'How wonderful, I can share all that is right with my husband. What more can I want?' But two further questions had to be asked: 'Are all non-believers anonymous Christians?'; and, 'If it is possible to follow Christ as an anonymous Christian, why proclaim the Gospel?'

ARE ALL NON-BELIEVERS ANONYMOUS CHRISTIANS?

Rahner answers this question by saying that, by virtue of the grace of Christ, which is at least a constant offer, every human being is always in a Christ-determined situation, whether he or she has accepted this grace or not. However, it is better not to call this 'Christian' position on the part of every human being 'implicit' or 'anonymous' Christianity straight away. Otherwise we might obscure the radical distinction between *grace offered* and *grace accepted* in faith and love.[14]

In other words, in order to be called an anonymous Christian a man or woman has to accept the promptings of grace in their lives and act on them. Such thoughts are a great comfort for the believer in a marriage, but they also carry with them the temptation to think that anonymous Christianity might be enough.

That is why the second question has to be asked.

IF ANONYMOUS CHRISTIANITY IS POSSIBLE, WHY PROCLAIM THE GOSPEL?

Speaking about the Sacraments, Archbishop Weakland has said that there is an erroneous approach, attributed falsely to Karl Rahner, that Sacraments only celebrate what is found in nature or in one's life. For people who believe this, the Sacraments add nothing.[15]

In the context of anonymous Christianity, it would be possible to draw the mistaken conclusion that coming to explicit belief in Christ, and hence the proclamation of the Gospel, do not matter. In other words, if there is nothing to add to anonymous Christianity, then there seems little point in evangelisation, or, in a marriage, wishing for the other person to become an explicit Christian.

Rahner hit this temptation on the head in a talk he gave to a group of Bavarian Catholics, in which he spoke about the temptation not to do all one can to help other people get to know Christ.

> The ultimate depth of grace is revealed in this, that God lets good come of evil. But woe to that man who thinks that this means he can usurp God's position; that he can do evil that good may come. Woe to that man who thinks that he can outwit God. But this is what we should be trying to do if we made the possibility of salvation outside God's normal means of salvation into a basis for the conclusion that we have no apostolic task, or no urgent one: this sense of being responsible for my brother, not only for his earthly needs but precisely for his eternal salvation, may be nothing short of decisive for my own eternal salvation.[16]

Speaking a little more formally of the possible transition from anonymous to explicit Christianity, Rahner says that anonymous Christianity always strives towards its full name, towards an explicit expression. Unfavourable historical conditions may hinder this full expression, so that it does not go beyond the appearance of loving humanness.

But, Rahner says, an anonymous Christian will always react with openness

> . . . whenever a new and higher stage of explicitness is presented to him right up to the ultimate perfection of a consciously accepted profession of Church membership. Here alone does this belief find not merely its greatest support and source of confidence but also its proper reality and that peace which St Augustine likened to repose in being: peace and repose which do not mean stagnation and flight but the capacity of casting oneself all the more resolutely into the inexorable will of the mystery of God, since now, as St Paul says, one knows whom one believes and to whom one fearlessly submits in radical trust.[17]

At the age of eighty, in the last year of his life, Karl Rahner gave an interview in which he was asked about the anonymous Christian.

> You see, what it means is terribly simple and straightforward. Whether one should use the label 'anonymous Christianity' or not is something one can argue about. What is meant is that someone who follows his own conscience, whether he thinks he should be a Christian or not, whether he thinks he should be an atheist, or not, is accepted before God and by God, and can reach that eternal life we confess in our Christian faith as the goal of all. In other words, grace and justification, relationship and union with God, and the possibility of attaining eternal life are only limited by a person's bad conscience. And that is in fact what the term 'anonymous Christianity' tries to say.[18]

Love demands of me that I must be willing to be the instrument through which another person, the person I am closest to, can become more fully himself. But it also demands that I should not have an 'agenda', or, at any rate, that the 'agenda' should be God's, not mine.

Avoiding the Cross

There is an Intercession in the Morning Prayer of the Church, which says, 'You, Lord, are the sole master of the future: keep us from despair and the fear of what is to come.'[19]

It is natural to wish to control the future, especially when there is something you very much want, something which is in itself good, such as your spouse coming to belief in Christ. When I was first married, I thought that, if I could only get my husband to go to church with me a few times, then faith would automatically be the result, and we would be able to share much more. I did persuade him to go a few times, but he came unwillingly, felt very uncomfortable and I think my thinly veiled 'waiting for the conversion to happen' was probably the last straw for him. These visits to church led to anything but sharing so I stopped asking him to come. I have learnt, since, that there is a temptation called 'Trying to help the holy Spirit along'!

How, then, am I to achieve the balance between proclaiming (sharing!) my faith and not trying to engineer a conversion? In the course of my marriage I have slowly learnt that the less I pushed, the more open would my husband become to talking about religious issues. What was required of me was not just 'not pushing', but a complete openness, which did not permit me to think, with even the smallest part of my mind, that 'I was achieving a conversion.' I am reminded here of the openness required in prayer. The initiative is God's, not mine. What He asks of me is the readiness to act at His prompting.

I was very much helped by a comment at a parish meeting to the effect that the temptations of Christ in the desert were all invitations to hurry the 'hour', to force the Father's hand, to avoid the tension and pain of patiently awaiting the right time and the right way for the completion of His ministry. They were temptations to avoid the Cross.[20]

In the case of a marriage where one partner is waiting, hoping that the 'hour' of belief will come for the other partner too, giving in to such a temptation would mean having greater regard for one's own comfort than for that of the other person. It would mean forgetting that, in many areas of His life on earth, Christ, too, shared in the suffering of 'not knowing' and that He said of his Second Coming 'that as for that hour, nobody knows it, neither the angels of heaven, nor the Son, no one but the Father only.'[21]

'Not knowing' is one way of following Christ.

Openness to the other person

Not knowing implies openness, in this case openness as regards my husband's coming to belief. Rahner's comments about the attitude of Christians to non-Christians are particularly helpful.

> From what has been said . . . about anonymous Christianity, as being the very opposite to an understanding of Christianity as an ideology, it follows then that there must be a similar attitude of positive tolerance towards non-Christians; this tolerance distinguishes the firmness and missionary zeal of the Faith from the fanaticism which is and must be characteristic of an ideology because only by such fanaticism can an ideology safeguard its strict boundaries against the greater reality surrounding it; *Christianity in contrast is of its very nature commanded to look for itself in the other and to trust that it will once more meet itself and its greater fullness in the other.*[22]

That this fullness has not in the past meant, and may not in the future mean, that everyone will come to belief in Christ is, in my view, the most painful tension for the Church in today's world. In the private sphere, a Christian married to a non-believer lives this tension in daily life. Knowing that Christ is already at work in many of those outside the Church can make this a fruitful tension and an invitation to dialogue.

A Marriage 'Like the Church in the World'

When Pope John Paul II visited the UK in 1982, he spoke to couples living in 'inter-church marriages' saying that in their married lives they lived all the hopes and difficulties facing the Christian Churches on their path to unity.[23] In a similar way a marriage between a Christian and a non-believer mirrors the situation of the Church in the world and here, too, the Christian as well as the non-believer can benefit from the dialogue. I know that I have been brought closer to God though the influence of my non–believing spouse.

The parallel with the relationship between the Church and the world is made clear in the Vatican II document, 'The Church in the World Today'. It stresses not only the role of the Church as a social reality and driving force in history, but also emphasises how much the Church itself has benefited from scientific progress and the wealth of cultures in the world, ' . . . through which greater light is thrown on the nature of man and *new avenues to truth are opened up.*'[24]

The dialogue is not a one-way process. In proclaiming the Word to the world and trying to share my Christian faith with my husband, I can only do so with humility, knowing how much I have to learn from him – just as the Church is aware how much it can benefit from contact with the world.

The 'Good Friday Intercessions' again

As I am writing this, another Good Friday has passed, and I have listened to the Intercessions once more: 'Let us pray for those who do not believe in God, that they may find him by sincerely following all that is right.'

This year, as we reached this Intercession, I realised that it had a new, and more profound, meaning for me. As I heard the words of this prayer, I was deeply moved, and pain was only part of what I felt. I now know that it is possible to pray this Intercession not just as a prayer for those at the edge of the Church, but also as a prayer for those who are already, by the way they live, at the centre of the Church – even if they themselves do not and may never know it.

On future Good Fridays I trust I will be able to pray the Intercessions with a new openness, borne of the awareness that I do not, finally, know who is closest to Christ and who is furthest away, that the concentric circles around Him are not static. Some of those closest to Christ do not appear in the visible structure of the Church. They are what Karl Rahner calls anonymous Christians.

Summary

FOR NON-BELIEVERS

This chapter reflects on the goodness and love of neighbour which I as the Christian marriage partner see in my non-believing husband.

There can be no Christianity without love of neighbour and this is so important that the theologian Karl Rahner describes someone who lives in neighbourly love as an anonymous Christian, though he or she would not refer to themselves in this way. Sharing love of neighbour with my husband is one way in which I can share my Christian faith in action with someone who does not believe. This sharing is not a conversion attempt, but a wish to share all that can be shared. I have learnt that all talk about the faith must respect the integrity of the other person. In this way there can be a fruitful shared life and dialogue between couples like us, similar to the positive dialogue between the Church and the world that Church documents from Vatican II invite.

FOR BELIEVERS

Almost at the end of the Good Friday Intercessions there is a prayer, for those who do not believe in God, but who seek to do *all that is right*, which means a great deal to me. Many people who do not believe in Christ (or God) are 'Christians by behaviour'. Rahner's description of someone who follows Christ without knowing Him as an anonymous Christian has helped me to live my Christian faith in my marriage with a non-believer. Good though this is, I have realised that it may lead to a temptation to think that anonymous Christianity may be enough (no need for mission). Alternatively, I may, as a Christian, feel tempted to try to 'hurry the hour' (of belief) for the non-believer. Everyone is called to the fullness of faith, but there are good people, who do not come to belief. No one knows another person's 'hour', so for me walking in openness, 'not knowing', has become one way of following Christ.

FOR CLERGY

This chapter has considered the implications for a Christian of marriage to a non-believer in the light of the Good Friday Intercessions and Karl Rahner's concept of the anonymous Christian. The idea of the anonymous Christian can be an inspiration for Christians living such a marriage, as it helps them see Christ outside the Church (as has been the case for me). It is an essential part of being a Christian to wish to share faith, but it is important to carry out the command to mission with openness and respect for the other person's integrity, as I have learnt through my marriage. Just as an inter-Church marriage mirrors the situation between the Churches, so a marriage between a Christian and a non-believer (such as my own) mirrors the situation of the Church in the world and therefore has its own distinctive contribution to make to the living of the Christian faith today.

CHAPTER FIVE

Growing Together I

A knowledge of human affairs, too, must be acquired, which is so useful even to a theologian, that without it he may perhaps sing pleasantly to himself, but will certainly not sing agreeably to the people.

St Thomas More[1]

The brethren should serve one another, with no one being excused from kitchen service except on the grounds of illness or because engaged in some important business; for such service secures a richer recompense and greater love.

St Benedict[2]

When I first met my husband the science/arts difference was not the only one between us. There were differences in nationality, religion and also social background. Many 'tacit assumptions' were therefore different and this required adjustments for both of us.

Being abroad is normal

The most familiar objects I can remember from my childhood are the striking Roman oil lamps that I saw in nearly every home on my mother's side of the family. The lamps are tall brass structures to which are attached implements for pulling up the wicks and for cleaning the oil burners. I now have one at home and I have given one to my daughter too. The lamps were brought back from Italy by my German grandmother and her sisters, who had spent several years there with their widowed mother. The family had been living in Berlin, the girls were ailing after moving from the country and a doctor suggested that 'a change of air' might help. Not being a woman of half measures, my great-grandmother took her daughters on an extended 'tour' of Europe and North Africa, during which my grandmother met my Danish grandfather.

My mother's brother and sister both worked, and had married, abroad — and I think perhaps most significantly for the future direction of my life, my mother had trained as a kindergarten teacher in London and retained a great affection for 'all things English'. This included the language, which was regularly spoken in my parent's home. I cannot remember a time when I have not known at least some English.

So travelling and living abroad, was normal in my family. During my teens, I began to think that not only did I want to read English at university but also had a growing feeling that I was meant to live in the UK; this seemed a perfectly natural development to me.

A Church of many languages

One of the first things I noticed about the Church in the UK was the fact that nearly all the priests I came into contact with spoke fluent English. Coming from a country where most priests were 'imported' and therefore spoke accented or broken Danish, my immediate reaction was one of total disbelief: 'another native priest!'

In the tiny Roman Catholic community in Copenhagen where I had grown up, not only were most of the priests from other countries, but the church where I went to mass as a child drew a sizeable part of its congregation from the diplomatic community.

Many of the 'Danish' members, including myself, were, at least partly, of foreign origin, the local sisters were mainly French and sermons were regularly preached in French and English. As most of the mass was still in Latin, the Catholic Church as I then knew it gave a distinct impression of being a foreign implant. However, my own dominant impression during those years was one of the Catholic Church as a world Church. Latin was the language of the universal Church, many nationalities went to mass, all belonging to the same Church.

As I began to learn foreign languages at school, I also began to enjoy trying to understand the sermons in French and English and following the Latin mass in the original. My life-long interest in languages was nourished in the Church in which I grew up, and English was one of the languages used in that Church.

So I grew up with a strong sense of belonging in a universal Church, one that looked across national borders and appeared to me as not really a part of the Danish 'scene'. I am sure that the idea was instilled into me, subconsciously at least, that practising my religion was likely to entail some degree of isolation from the society in which I lived. Since I accepted this as 'normal', it did not worry me and may well have helped prepare me for marriage to a non-believer and life (as for many other Christians now), in a largely post-Christian society.

On leaving school I took the opportunity to spend a year in England. The friendship I made with the family I stayed with eventually led to my gaining a research post at Keele. My feeling that I was meant to spend the rest of my life in the UK had indeed come true, but that did not mean that everything was now plain sailing.

A very English background

Where my background had been international, both in Church and family terms and where I had grown up with the notion that being, and living, in a country other than the one I had been born in was normal, my husband came from a very different background.

As far as I know, all his forebears are English, having mainly come from East Anglia where he had grown up; the 'religious context' was that of the Anglican Church.

Some of his relatives had lived and worked in English-speaking 'Commonwealth' countries but neither of his parents had trained, or worked, abroad. Where I had imbibed foreign languages from childhood, his attention had been turned in different directions and I get the impression that he was always more interested in 'how things work'. There was a chemistry set in the garden shed – and, I gather, various explosions at the bottom of the garden! At a later stage he got to know about car engines, he made small pieces of furniture and he learnt about growing things in the garden. Some of these skills he learnt from his parents, but he departed from his surroundings by discovering that he enjoyed opera, that he loved walking in the mountains and that he wished to go to university, where he met and made friends with students from other countries.

Where my background had conditioned me to look abroad, but had perhaps been lacking in national 'rootedness', my husband's background had given him a sense of rootedness within a specific area and he was now beginning to be ready to look further afield.

Getting to know each other

My husband recently said about one of his students, 'He will have to decide what it is he really wants out of life. If he doesn't know that, I don't see how he can make the right decisions.' When we were getting to know each other, we spent many hours finding out what was important in life for each of us.

When we met, my husband had just bought the largest (and best-made) loudspeakers I have ever seen; too big for his flat, really, but what he cared about was the quality of the sound they produced. This was not the flat he was going to be in for the rest of his life, so he had bought ahead, but he also acquired a few smaller things, to make the flat a bit more pleasing to the eye. I remember a colourful tablecloth, which covered the rather 'distressed' coffee table. I began to form a picture of someone who cared about his surroundings, who appreciated beauty, who was prepared to wait – who thought at length before he did anything; someone who needed to see the evidence for what he believed.

I too appreciated beautiful things, but in a different way: pictures, antique furniture, (cut) flowers. I think I was more interested in the appearance of beautiful things than in their construction. I, too, was looking for evidence in my linguistic research, but I was also aware that there were other areas, those belonging to theological thought, where weighing, measuring and counting of occurrences, were not the only appropriate methods of observation.

Our differences led us to reflect very carefully on whether we had enough in common. There were times when the decision whether to marry or not seemed to hang in the balance. It certainly never felt as if marriage was the inevitable 'next step' in our relationship and it may be that the differences between us made for a much more considered commitment.[3]

When I think of this now, I cannot help remembering someone I came across long before I met my husband. I had spent some time reflecting on the fundamental shape my life was going to take and had reached the conclusion that the married state was the right one for me. This, of course, left the question of who I was going to marry! Clearly it was going to be a case of waiting and seeing and it was at this stage that a friend described an acquaintance of hers: a Catholic arts academic. It sounded as if we might have something in common and I remember wondering, in passing, whether this was perhaps the man I was meant to marry. Later, we happened to be at the same function and I have never, ever, met anyone I had less in common with! I am sure he was a good man, but we had nothing to say to each other. This chance meeting has stayed with me as an example of how dangerous it is to try to work out in advance whether two people are going to get on together, whether in marriage or in other contexts.

As it turned out, there were considerable differences between my future husband and myself: he was in science, I was in the arts;

he came from a 'one-country' background, mine was more international; he had never believed in God, I had always been a believer. However, there were shared interests and attitudes. We both had a reflective approach to life, we were analytical in our areas of research and we appreciated beauty, even if not always of the same kind. From our very different 'starting points' we began to share our thoughts and our stories, each adding a new dimension to what the other was able to provide. As the believer I, in a sense, became my (future) husband's 'theologian' and he, for his part, drew my attention to aspects of the natural world which I had not considered before.

I do not think that the reasons for love can be reduced to observable facts only. Shared interests and attitudes are important, but they are not the whole story. For me the question of vocation[4] came into it: I felt called to marriage, and I felt called to marry this particular man. Religious motivation obviously did not come into the decision for him, but I think we both felt that there came a time when we had evaluated as much as we could and that the next step was the joint decision to commit ourselves to a future together, in marriage.

Until I met my husband my appreciation of nature had been largely limited to its more 'civilised' aspects: I enjoyed good views, a well laid-out garden, beautiful flowers. I had been on one walking holiday with friends, which had been highly enlightening, but at the age of eighteen I don't think it had yet dawned on me that hill walking was something one might enjoy!

We began to go walking together while we were both at Keele. A few sunny days in the Peak District doing some gentle walking with friends, and seeing butterflies galore, made me want to try again. Soon after we were married and had moved to Swansea I bought some decent walking boots. It was while trying them out in the Wye Valley that I got stuck in a fence. We were following a footpath with a fence across it and the only way to get through was by scrambling along the ground. The only problem was that I had forgotten how to move my body in that way! As we went for more walks, I discovered not only that there was a sense of achievement in getting to my destination, but that I felt a sense of joy in just moving my body along a path and sometimes in each individual step of a small scramble.

Our first walks together were in the UK, but after a few years we thought we could afford a holiday in the Austrian Alps. This was scenery on a different scale, both in comparison with the flat Danish countryside I had been used to, but also for my husband, who had not walked in mountains of this height before. I think it stretched both of us: going abroad was something I was used to (and I did speak some German, which helped both of us) and scrambling up rather large mountains held no terrors for my husband. When we were back home he said how glad he was that I had persuaded him to go. And I felt my horizons had been expanded.

When we were first married money was short. We had just enough to buy a house but not to furnish it. So we started with a few essentials like a bed and a kitchen table and gradually made other things. The art of building slowly did not come easily to me even though, as a student, I had known what it is like to walk round a supermarket looking for something to eat that is both nourishing and affordable. On the other hand, the art of living with very little money was one in which my husband was well schooled.

While we were waiting for the (new) house to be ready and spending a few days in a boarding house, my husband started assembling a lampshade kit we had bought earlier. It was the one bit of building he could do from where we were, and he did it. I learnt that one did not have to sit down and wait during a hold-up, one simply got on with what was possible at the time, however small the progress might seem.

Other 'construction projects' followed and I began to have ideas too: the bookcase he built while I was away sitting my final exams in Copenhagen was painted black at my suggestion. 'It looked dead in all black,' he told me when I got back, 'but then it came to life when I put all the books in.'

Most of our furniture was built in this way – and it took time. It was only years later, when we could afford things ready made and we bought a table, that I felt a sense of disappointment. The, sometimes slow, process of assembly had had a value in itself. While we patiently made things together, we had also been growing together as a couple and what we produced had been one way of bearing fruit. I now know how much love we put into these first efforts at creating a home and, in a small way, this appeared to me like God putting His love, and His patience, into the work of Creation.

My sister-in-law, who enjoys growing plants, once commented that few people now grew plants from seed. They liked just buying a plant in flower and then threw it out when it had finished flowering. 'There is a value in caring for a plant,' she said, 'and in waiting for it to flower. You lose that if you just buy the plant in flower and throw it out afterwards.'

Furnishing a house can be a satisfying activity, the 'maintenance' involved in any household is quite another matter, at least as far as I am concerned. A fellow researcher once told me that he had discussed the relative values of getting married and 'living together' with some of his students (who felt that 'living together' was much more glamorous) and he had said, 'OK, so you go and live together and what happens? You'll run out of food and someone will have to remember to buy some and the washing-up will pile up in the kitchen and will have to be dealt with – and one of you might actually mind about the fluff under sofa . . . '

I think my colleague was trying to instil some sense of reality into those starry-eyed young couples who thought that if you did not get married somehow all the boring aspects of sharing a household would go away. They do not, of course. Setting up any kind of home entails the manual work involved in cleaning and cooking and gardening and general upkeep.

Our marriage has gone through different phases as far the 'division of labour' is concerned. Before our daughter arrived we did most of the manual tasks together, while she was small I did most of the 'indoor' tasks, and now we are sharing again. That does not mean that we have now simply returned to square one.

'In the beginning' I thought that any kind of manual labour was a waste of time, at any rate a waste of *my* time and I shared what had to be done very unwillingly. I am sure that must have made it difficult for my husband and, in retrospect, I think I was creating a quite unnecessary barrier between us. It would have been wrong to ask a spouse to pretend to have faith when he did not, but anyone can approach a task they do not like in a spirit of service – and it took me a long time to learn that.

During the early years of our marriage we did all the cooking and cleaning together on Saturdays. The cooking was enjoyable, I think, for both of us – it was creative – but I never enjoyed cleaning the house. In fact, I found it so unpleasant that, when I did more of it by myself after our daughter arrived, I decided to do it on Fridays, when Catholics are encouraged to do something (a 'penance') which unites them with the suffering of Christ on Good Friday. (I would now consider my motivation for this choice of penance highly suspect!)

As our daughter has grown older, and my work has expanded again, we have gradually shifted the cleaning back to Saturday and are doing it together and it is now a shared task which I welcome. It was not until we had been married several years that I came across the Benedictine Rule, originally written as a way of life for monastic communities, but which many other people find helpful too. It was while reading other married womens' reflections on this Rule, that I discovered its emphasis on both (manual) work and prayer and began to see clearly the link between the two.[5] But even in those early days I realised that something happened to my relationship with my husband when we had worked together well at some demanding physical task.

In our first house, the back garden sloped steeply upwards and had a lot of rocks in it. We, or rather my husband, had the idea of dividing the garden into levels, with a paved path running along the top. For this he suggested that we should use some of the rocks we had dug out while constructing the lower levels. I think it was while we were constructing this path that I began to try to do this kind of work in a rather better spirit.

I had not grown up with a garden and had no real interest, then, in growing plants, or planning the layout of a garden. However, I tried to help him with this grand design and I even did a small section by myself, using a spirit level and fitting the stones together to make a smooth path. Until I came to write this I had completely forgotten how pleased my husband was that I should have tried to show some interest in making a garden. It is only now that I realise how alone he must have felt when wanting to do tasks like that and seeing no interest from me at all. If I felt alone spiritually, then he must have felt alone, a lot of the time, in his 'home-making' projects and in his interest in the physical surroundings in which we lived.

The world crying out to be loved

I have mentioned how hard it is to be unable to share one's faith with one's spouse, but in writing this, I have come to realise that the desire for sharing, and the pain when this does not happen, does not concern spiritual matters alone. There is a tendency among some Christians (including myself in the early days of our marriage) to despise the physical world in which we live, as unworthy of people with their minds on higher (spiritual!) matters. This attitude is clearly hurtful to anyone, whether Christian or not, working hard to make the best use of the materials to hand, but it must be particularly hurtful for the non-believer in a marriage with a Christian, because it is as if the Christian is saying to the partner, 'Your world, the only world that you know, does not matter to me, or not nearly as much as "my" spiritual world.' This is, of course, a totally unbiblical attitude and I have come to realise that it is not a matter of 'either/or', but of 'both/and'.

A priest once told me that even hermits, who have withdrawn almost completely from contact with the world, need to attend to practical tasks! St Francis of Assisi arranged for the hermit members of his order sometimes to take the place of the brothers who provided for their practical needs 'as from time to time it may seem good to them to exchange roles.'[6]

Practical tasks most certainly have their place within the God-given scheme of things and I now know that it is not good for

anyone to be completely exempt from them. However, that was all
in the future in the early days of our marriage. For the time being I
was only too happy when I could get out of the manual work in our
home. It never occurred to me that I was thereby neglecting part
of the creation which God loves so much and which St Paul speaks
of in a particularly loving and compassionate way, when he says
that it 'is eagerly waiting to enjoy the same glory and freedom as the
children of God.'[7]

When Christians do not love the world as they are meant to,
then, not only are they not serving their Creator as they should, but
their witness to those who do not yet believe in God is incomplete.
I now see that nothing, except evil, should be excluded from the
care and loving attention of a believer in Christ and that it is precisely in this loving attention that Christians and non-believers can
come together in a joint purpose. This is especially true of a marriage between a Christian and a non-believer, but it took me a long
time even to begin to realise that there was something to be learnt.[8]

God's spirit at work

In spite of the difficulties, we were beginning to grow together.
The reaching out for new experiences that had begun in both of us
before we met was making itself more and more felt. I was now
enjoying mountain walking, my husband was beginning to enjoy
other countries and higher mountains and I was beginning to
realise that manual work was not all toil, but could be a way of
growing in love. We were, however tentatively, moving into each
other's worlds.

Looking back, it seems to me that there was a spiritual aspect to
our striving to understand each other's worlds, especially through
the manual work we did together. I am sure that the work my husband did with so much good will had its part in the building of the
Kingdom. For me, this work together increasingly became a turning to God, another kind of prayer. I was discovering, with St

Benedict, that such service leads to greater love and that the Spirit of Love is powerfully present in such circumstances. I was later to discover that it is precisely this 'devotion to his material duties and the demands made upon him by the persons under his care' that Karl Rahner singles out as one of the distinguishing features of his anonymous Christians. Such a description is, necessarily, framed from the standpoint of faith. By their very nature, anonymous Christians could not describe themselves as such. But from my point of view, I was realising that in the service of shared work and in the 'devotion to material duties' believers and non-believers can be united in love.

Summary

FOR NON-BELIEVERS

This chapter describes the background from which my husband and I started. It shows how our respective gifts and limitations have shaped us in a way that, in retrospect, seems to have prepared us for this kind of marriage. It shows, also, our reflections on whether we had enough in common. For me to appreciate the hard physical work my non-believing husband put into making a home took a long time. If I felt alone in my Christianity, he must have felt isolated when 'labouring' alone. The chapter goes on to show how we began to grow together through sharing activities for which we did not initially have an inclination, thereby widening each other's horizons.

FOR BELIEVERS

The early stages of 'growing together' have been outlined, with an emphasis on the value of patience learnt particularly through perseverance in manual work. I learnt this kind of patience from my non-believing husband. I reflect on how the world is crying out to be cared for and freed to serve God and how the negative attitude of some Christians (including myself) to the more wearisome aspects of the material world, is a counter-witness to the loving purpose of God for the world. Through my own experience I have found that, by valuing and caring for creation together, Christians and non-believers can grow in love for each other too.

FOR CLERGY

In this chapter I describe the 'natural' starting points for my marriage. It shows how differences can be an enrichment as well as a difficulty. People of similar qualities and background do not necessarily 'match'. From the Christian point of view I see my marriage as a vocation and my decision to marry this particular man as a stepping forward, in faith, into the unknown. St Benedict's view of the value of shared manual work and Karl Rahner's description of the devotion to duty of the anonymous Christian have both inspired me. They show me that, in caring for Creation, believing and non-believing marriage partners serve God jointly, though they undertake this service from very different standpoints.

CHAPTER SIX

Work

You need not see what someone is doing
to know if it is his vocation,

you have only to watch his eyes:
a cook mixing a sauce, a surgeon

making a primary incision,
a clerk completing a bill of lading,

wear the same rapt expression,
forgetting themselves in a function . . .

W. H. Auden[1]

Man's work . . . cannot consist in the mere exercise of
human strength . . . It must leave room for man to prepare
himself by becoming more and more what in the will of
God he ought to be, for 'the rest' that the Lord reserves for
his servants and friends.

Pope John Paul II[2]

I cannot remember a time when I have not been interested in language: how languages relate to each other, the ways in which different languages express the same idea, the structure and sound
and intonation of a new language.

Others must have noticed this in me. Some friends took me out on the river in Cambridge and a boat bearing people who looked as if they might be Chinese passed us. Snatches of their conversation floated towards our boat.

One of my friends said, 'Look at Anita imbibing a new language.'

She was quite right. I had been intently listening to the sounds of this unfamiliar language.

There is, I think, a link between my interest in language and my Church work which now occupies most of my time. Both are to do with ordering things and relating them to each other. This is something I have only come to see fairly recently. Indeed, I was taken totally aback when someone said to me at an event I was organising, 'This is a true ministry!'

It certainly seems to be something I can do and, as a friend said, 'You do it in the service of *people*.'

A third strand to my working life, or, should I say, working ability, was highlighted for me during a meal with friends. I was talking to a woman writer (married with a large family) and I asked her, 'When do you find time to write?'

She said, 'I write whenever I can, often early in the morning.'

I knew then, though I did not say so, that I too wanted to write, other things than the thesis and the occasional short pieces I had done so far. The only question was when.

Over the years there have been tensions and shifts of emphasis between these three strands. Administration has dominated for many years, the writing is beginning to emerge, and my interest in language, though I do not imagine I will ever use it 'professionally' again, still makes itself felt, sometimes in unexpected places.

The common feature between these strands is, I think, an ability to organise, whether it is linguistic material, putting on a course and communicating information to others, or marshalling the facts and reflections that go into a piece of writing.

Structure and planning come into all of these activities and this is where my husband, the scientist, and I, the English language researcher, first began to find common ground. As a marriage counsellor once pointed out to me, even opposites need to find common ground.

Sharing skills

I may have the talent to organise but it was my husband who helped me develop it. His interest in the use of computers in chemical research had led him to switch from chemistry to computing and, to begin with, I did not see any specific link between his work and my own. However, the linguistic research I was doing at the time involved counting occurrences of Old English structures and this required searching through the texts which was a slow and laborious process. When I mentioned this to my husband he suggested that I might like to use a computer to do the initial sort through the texts and I thought it was worth a try.

Using a computer for linguistic research certainly taught me something about its potential – and also its limitations. For instance, slight variations in spelling that I would have picked up without thinking about it were not picked up by the computer. On the other hand, using the computer's search and find facility cut out much repetitive work and hence was worth doing. More important from the point of view of our relationship was that my husband had the ability to look creatively at what I was doing, in a very different area of work. He was reaching into my world, and offering me something from his own.

How I managed to pass O-level maths I do not know. But I do remember the relief with which I left numbers behind – forever, as I thought. Given a more encouraging home environment, I might not have developed the trouble with numbers that has dogged me for much of my life. As it was, I got into the habit of 'blanking out' as soon as someone mentioned anything to do with numbers. This was a handicap when my husband was trying to tell me about his work – which tended to involve numbers, one way or another.

In the early stage of our marriage when he told me about his latest ideas I would be wondering, 'Why is he boring me with this?'

A lesser man would have stopped talking altogether, but he kept trying. Eventually, I reached a stage where I could listen, even though the automatic 'blanking-out' at the beginning of the conversation often meant that I had to ask him to repeat things.

My block about anything numerical had become so 'matter-of-course' that it took me a long time to realise the reason for it. I eventually came to see that I associated numbers with childhood put-downs ('Any idiot could do this sum. It's easy . . . '). Once I had realised this and talked to my husband about it, the 'blanking out' did not happen quite so much. I will never be able to follow the finer points, but I can now see that my husband's mathematical ability is a gift rather than a threat.

New perspectives

When we moved to Swansea, I wanted to carry on doing research. But, by that time, I was beginning to wonder whether or not I should continue with linguistic research. One of the requirements for my Copenhagen MA (apart from the thesis) had been a sustained piece of work on a group of writers of social or religious importance. I chose a group who had written on the sixteenth- and seventeenth-century 'Ideal of the Christian Gentleman'.

This work I found to be so interesting that I considered it for my PhD – especially as it was more people-oriented than studying language structure – but I was advised against it. The field was crowded, I was told, and there was no one to supervise me.

I therefore carried on with my linguistic research, but the wish to move into an area that was rather more directly involved with people stayed with me. For the time being, however, I did research into Old English syntax, helped to some extent by the use of a computer, but also with a niggling worry that counting occurrences of structures meant handling and interpreting figures. Up to a point I could do it, but my ability was, and is, limited.

I might have continued with linguistic research but was brought up sharp when my thesis was 'referred', which meant that I had to rewrite it to get it accepted. About the same time I found I was expecting our daughter. It was time to think and to consider my options.

The MA degree I had done in Copenhagen was aimed at those seeking a job in university teaching and research and this was the kind of work I had imagined for myself. When I married and moved to the UK, this was still how I saw my working life developing and I started the PhD with a view to being better qualified for a British university post. Looking back, I suppose this was a very narrow aim, but it was the one thing that I wanted to do and for which I thought I had the ability. Also, in the 1970s, the job situation had not yet got as difficult as it would become later on. It never occurred to me that there might not be a job at the end of all this training.

Marriage did not change my assumption that I would do research and university teaching, in some form, as soon as I had finished my PhD. Already, I was applying for jobs within reasonable reach of Swansea but when my thesis was referred it did not improve my chances of getting the kind of post I was looking for! In any case, there was now a third person to consider.

It had always been my intention that, if and when we had children, I would carry on working. This would be part-time, as I felt it important that I be with our child for a substantial part of the day. We had existed on my husband's salary (amplified by the small grant I had been awarded) for the first part of our marriage. Since we were able to survive on one income, I had the option of considering part-time work without worrying too much about the amount of money it would bring in. However, I now had a thesis to rewrite, which would effectively become my (unpaid) part-time work. So we decided that, for the time being, I would spend such working time as I had on finishing the thesis, fitting it around looking after the baby when it arrived.

Naturally, I also spent time considering my long-term options. If I was going to carry on doing research, and also doing some teaching, what were my chances of doing so part-time?

Pondering my future (and by this time our daughter had been born), I went to mass one Sunday morning and felt 'disgusted' with the sermon. The preacher had spoken about adult religious education (I cannot now remember the details) and I went to see him afterwards about something which I felt 'just wasn't good enough'.

'And what are you doing about it?' he said.

I am sure he was not trying to make me feel guilty. He was simply pointing out that everyone in the Church has a responsibility for what goes on. He had also thrown down a gauntlet.

The preacher's question probably fed my thoughts about moving into a more 'human interest' area of work. Instead of returning to my earlier idea of doing research on the 'Ideal of the Christian Gentleman', I began to consider working for the Church. Theology had always been a strong interest and it occurred to me that it might be possible to do this kind of work part-time and locally.

Meanwhile, I had the viva for my PhD to face. This time the external examiner was a theologian who had done research into New Testament Greek. At the end of the viva (which I passed!) he asked me what I was going to do next. Looking at the bookcase behind him, with its king-sized Bible the sight of which had sustained me throughout the viva, I told him that I was planning to work in adult religious education for the Catholic Church. I had picked up the gauntlet.

Working for free

The Catholic Church was, at this stage, blissfully unaware of my intentions and I myself was not entirely sure how I was going to go about turning planning into action. In many ways it was like stepping into a void.

I realised, of course, that I now needed another form of training. Having read books on theology 'as and when' was not going to be enough. With a young child I could not very well go away to train, so I set about looking for correspondence courses. I eventually found a course leading to, what is now called, The Catholic Certificate in Religious Studies. This would involve at some stage a

Religious Education residential element and provide a qualification for working for the Church.

At that stage my enquiry of the Church as to the kind of work I had in mind was not encouraging. I was told that it was unlikely that any such work would be available and if it was it would not be paid. It was fortunate for me that my husband earned enough for us to live on and that he was happy for me to 'work for free'. But the reaction from 'the powers that be' made me realise that, especially given the constraints on my mobility, I was unlikely to end up with a 'job', even when I had more time to offer than was possible at that stage.

I now had some more specific choices to make and I decided to work for the Church (if it would accept me), to do the work part-time (for the time being anyway) and to work for free if that was the only way forward. My husband supported these choices with their implications for him, both financial (living on one, modest, income) and domestic (sharing the care for our daughter and some of the household tasks, since we were not going to have the money for paid child care or help in the house).

I am well aware that my choice to work part-time and for free while my daughter was young is one I would not have had if we, like many couples, had needed a second income. As it was, my unusual choice of work was made possible through my husband's full and wholehearted support.

Shortly after I had made the decision to offer my services to the Church, we moved to East Anglia. I arrived in Norwich with my eyes open for opportunities to do the work that I felt called to do, but without any real idea of how to begin.

With hindsight I suppose I would have gone about things differently. But at that stage I rather naively (but trusting in God too) assumed that the adult religious education scene was something one did if one felt called to it – and the 'official' Church was willing to accept the offer. Meanwhile, I unpacked the cases, found a playgroup for my daughter, and carried on with my correspondence course.

'Would you be willing to teach some of the children?', my parish priest said one day. That was not really what I had in mind. I do not think I am particularly gifted with children, but I very much wanted to be used, so I agreed. It certainly turned out to be a challenge to my imagination and my 'creative' side. I scoured the local Resource Centre for catechetical material and started a small children's group in my own dining room, with my daughter on my lap. I think the children enjoyed each other's company!

Some time later my parish priest made another visit. 'Would you like to do something for the local radio?' he said. This was another 'first', but this time for adults. The new local radio station wanted members of churches to write a 'Pause for Thought'. 'All right,' I said. 'If you will pray for me.' He must have done, because it went well and was the beginning of a long association with that station. However, he was not the only one who helped. I was not very confident to begin with, and many is the 'Pause' that my husband has read and improved. 'You can't say that. It sounds stodgy,' he would say. 'You're not writing a book, you're talking to people – in the middle of their breakfast.' I think the station benefited greatly from his advice!

The time came to go on the residential course that was the final part of my Religious Education course. During my absence my husband looked after our daughter. It was interesting to meet others involved in Religious Education, but it also brought home to me the fact that most of them worked and brought up children. It looked as if, whatever direction my life was going to take, I was not going to be part of a large group. The support of my husband was very precious.

After we had been in Norwich for a couple of years, I went to a big gathering at the Roman Catholic Cathedral, where one of the 'sideshows' was a display on adult religious education. I picked up a leaflet and wrote to the Religious Education adviser, offering my services. This time my offer was accepted. Later, when the adviser set up an adult religious education team in the Norwich Deanery (a group of parishes), I was asked to be part of it. I was pleased that I was beginning to be used and, as my daughter was by now at school, I had more time to give to this new work.

I was happy to have made a start at the work I wanted to do.

Not only did my husband not raise any objections to my working for the Church, but he actively supported me in many practical ways.

The first project I was asked to do (along with a group of others) was the production of a series of sound tapes for the sick and housebound. Apart from my limited radio work, I started from scratch. I helped devise the content of the tapes, organised recording sessions, and learnt about publicity – and about people. It was at this stage that I also began to learn about long-term planning, about deadlines and about reminding people what they had promised to do. I found that although my husband mostly did not understand the content of my work he was always willing to discuss my 'current project'. He did so with far more empathy than I had been able to show for his work in the earlier years of our marriage.

'If you want a busy person to do something, make it easy for them,' he once said. 'Draft *something* for them to approve, give them a form to fill in, be brief and clear.' All this seems obvious to me now, but at that stage it was a revelation. Looking back, I also realise that he was teaching me a way of loving my neighbour.

As I was given more work to do, using time well became increasingly important. To begin with, I took ages to write a script and increasingly I did not have 'ages'. There were times when I felt defeated and humiliated after sitting staring at a blank page for hours, thinking of one possibility after another, and dismissing them all. On one such occasion my husband said. 'Get it down somehow. Make a plan, and then write something. It's a lot easier to edit than to write from scratch.' This was not a skill I acquired immediately, but, over the years, I have got faster. I now know that his advice was not only about saving time, but about establishing trust, and overcoming fear. It was good advice.

Boundaries

When he married me, my husband thought he was marrying a Roman Catholic linguist with a strong interest in her religion.

Neither he nor I knew that I was going to end up working voluntarily for the Catholic Church. He had always been supportive of my religious practice, but this change in my working life meant that he now found himself called on to extend his support in new ways – and he has done so. For me, working for the Church means that my work is in that area of my life which my husband loyally supports, but does not understand. When I have felt a conflict of loyalty between work and family, the fact that the work is for the Church has made it more difficult.

At one half-term holiday, when our daughter was still quite young, a team member who had agreed to do some publicity rang me at the last moment. There were complications, could I possibly do the publicity after all? I generally worked during school hours, but because of the holiday I had my daughter and her friend to look after. Feeling that the publicity must go out on time, I said yes and somehow did it, but I now know that I should have said 'Too bad. It will have to go out late.'

Because the work I do is for the Church that does not mean that it should always take priority over other responsibilities. There are boundaries to establish, especially when one is working from home. I am not a Dickens fan, but do remember reading his description of a chaotic home where the wife does 'philanthropic' work and her family is totally neglected. I can't recall the precise reference, but the image of the chaotic household, where priorities and boundaries had not been established, has stayed with me as a useful 'balancing tool'.[3]

My husband's generous enabling makes me feel that it is doubly important for me to stick to the necessary boundaries between work and family. But there have also been occasions when he has pulled me back from excessive worry about 'taking something from him'. My work sometimes entails going out to evening meetings and returning late. On one occasion I felt almost sick with worry that I might be inconsiderate to a husband with a very heavy workload if I did not return home until after 11.00 at night. I also had some notion that he probably resented my being out, because it was for the Church. (How convoluted can one be!) At least I had the sense to ask him what he thought. 'Why should I mind?' he said. 'As long as it's not every night.'

Sharing each other's work

In recent years my work has involved arranging retreats and meetings on adult religious education in my Deanery. Of course, all of these events are spare-time activities for those who attend. That is the rub: with increasing pressure on everyone's time, attendance at such events is not always high and it can be disappointing to have a low turnout, after putting a lot of work into arranging them.

'We only got twenty and we were hoping for forty,' I said to my husband on one occasion.

'But are you really doing it for the numbers'? he asked.

I had to admit that this was not the main reason. I took his comments to the next team meeting and saw that his words struck home. Of course large numbers can be encouraging, but I was reminded of Karl Rahner's comment to a group of lay people:

> We are an association whose members help each other in the task of a living apostolate, but we must certainly realise . . . that this is always going to be an affair of the few rather than of many people.[4]

This search for quality rather than quantity is an integral part of my husband's character and it has profoundly affected my work. For him it is simply a matter of 'doing what is right' and he would not see it as a way of turning towards Christian belief. But when I hear him going to the heart of the matter, as he did with this retreat, I cannot help being reminded that 'anyone who has let himself be taken hold of by grace can be called with every right an "anonymous Christian".'[5]

It is not often that I have a chance to help my husband with his work. On the whole it is his skills that enrich my work, but there are occasions where I think I have contributed something. Two examples will suffice.

As a lecturer my husband deals with people and his role is, in part, a pastoral one. He often discusses the problems and decisions involved in his work with me (within the bounds of confidentiality, of course). Questions about motivation, the use of abilities, the extent to which one can help other people, frequently come up. We approach these problems from different standpoints, but there is a large shared area where we consider together what is right, what is human, and what is good.

I have learnt to use a computer as a 'super word processor' and also for simple spreadsheets, but in his research my husband deals with computer languages and what they are capable of expressing. Such languages are specialised ones, which do not have the range of 'natural' languages like English or French, but the principles applied to the study of what a language can do are similar. My husband was considering what could and could not be expressed in a particular computer language and I said, 'In a natural language you would do it like this . . . ', and he thanked me for the light my comment had thrown on his problem. Sharing sometimes happens when it is least expected.

Using a computer has become a link between my husband and myself and an 'enabling' tool for my work. It has also, on occasion, established a link between him and the 'official' Church. With the shortage of priests in the Roman Catholic Church, time saving devices are much appreciated, so a few years ago I was involved in organising a computer course for clergy. My husband offered to teach the course, assisted by a priest. The course was well attended and much enjoyed and I gather that a certain amount of pleasant conversation went on afterwards.

Conversation or dialogue is a good way of describing the help that I have received from my husband and that he has given to others in the Church. St Bernard of Clairvaux speaks of this dialogue of trust and need and help in the relationship between God and ourselves. He says that recurrent troubles make us turn to God and on each occasion we learn how kind He is. In this way our needs (and the help we receive) become 'a kind of language', which speaks with joy of 'the benefits of which they have taught us the value.'[6]

This language, at the human level, is one that has become very familiar in our marriage.

When I was doing language research I do not think it occurred to me that human interaction, or interaction with God, could be thought of as a 'language'. So, when I began to work for the Church, it seemed that I was leaving the linguistic part of my life behind. However, God wastes nothing. I now find that my ability to analyse structures is an asset in organisation and planning and an essential part of the writing process. It is also something that I can share and discuss with my husband – as is computing, which has become a link between his work interests and mine. But I think it is our joint interest in working for and with people that brings us closest together.

When I discuss my work with my husband, his words often come across to me as God's promptings – and I feel that God is at work in him. But I respect the fact that is not how he sees it and that he is not aware of any relationship with God.

During our trip to the French Alps we had celebrated our twenty-fifth wedding anniversary and also done a 'stocktaking': 'How were we going to spend the remainder of our lives? What was really important?' We were walking along one of the rocky mountain paths and had just crossed a stream on a rickety wooden bridge, when I brought up the subject of this book. 'I have always wanted to write,' I told him, 'and I have had this book in mind for a long time.'[7]

'Then go ahead, you've done all sorts of things in your life, but a book would be something you could point to and say, "I did that.".'

The three strands of my working life now seem to be coming together: language, administration and writing. This work, carried out in the service of the Church and enabled by my husband, has encouraged a dialogue which is shaping both him and me and which continues to bring us closer. The language of this dialogue is mutual help, at the human level and also at the spiritual, Christian, level, though here the dialogue is entered into from two very different perspectives.

Summary

FOR NON-BELIEVERS

Throughout my working life, in language research and, more recently, in administration and writing, my husband has acted as an 'enabler', though he does not understand or share the Christian belief that motivates much of my work. He is often the one who goes to 'the heart of the matter' when we discuss the human and technical problems that arise in my work. His knowledge of computing, which he has shared with me, has made much of my work possible as well as creating a link between us. Through his profound observations on my life and work he has helped bring me closer to the God whose mark I see in my husband's life too.

FOR BELIEVERS

Working in very different fields has presented a challenge for my husband and me to reach out to each other. In spite of difficulties, we have communicated not only across the science/arts divide, but also across a religious divide. Our shared interest in people brings us together and I am moved by the way my husband has supported my call to work for the Church, in moral and practical terms and also financially. During our marriage I have learnt that boundaries are especially important when the believing partner also works for the Church. I have discovered that putting God first does not mean putting Church work first in all circumstances. Talking about problems that arise is an essential way of making sure that boundaries between family and work are kept and that both partners share and understand the priorities that underpin them.

FOR CLERGY

I have been surprised at how much sharing is possible in a marriage where only one partner is a believer. My move from language research to working for the Church would not have been possible without my husband's constant support, which I value especially because he does not believe in God. I have found that a non-believer can teach a believer much about love of neighbour and trust in God and hence help the vocation of the believer. In the context of our marriage I have become increasingly aware that God is present in the language of mutual help and trust which links our initially very different areas of work.

CHAPTER SEVEN

Prayer

... when you pray, go to your private room and ... pray to
your Father who is in that secret place.

Mt 6:6

If, charmed by their beauty, they have taken things for God's
... And if they have been impressed by their power and
energy, let them deduce from these how much mightier is He
that has formed them, since through the grandeur and
beauty of the creatures we may, by analogy, contemplate their
Author.

Wis 13:3–5

One of the best holidays we have ever had was the ten days we
spent in the Haute-Savoie, walking in the mountains near
Chamonix. Before we went there, I looked at a map of the French
Alps and saw that the small lakeside town of Annecy, where St
Francis de Sales had been based as a bishop, was within reach of
Chamonix.

'I would like to visit his house and tomb,' I said to my husband.
'He has written an introduction to prayer for lay people that I find

particularly helpful. The place is worth seeing in its own right – like a "little Venice", I'm told.'

'In that case, let's try to go there,' he said.

When we arrived in Annecy, my husband said, with his unerring sense of what is really important to me, 'Let's go to the tomb first.' We (he!) found the Basilica and while I was still peering around the dimly lit interior, he said, 'Look, there's the tomb, over there, by the altar.' And then he stood aside while I prayed.

This incident is typical of his whole attitude to 'the things of God' in my life. He knows that prayer is important to me – and, in a strange place, he is usually the first to discover where the Roman Catholic church is, so that I can go to mass, or, as in this case, visit the tomb of a saint who is special to me.

Family prayer

Praying in a church is one thing, praying at home is another.

'After we are married, how will I be able to pray?' I asked a priest. 'For instance, how will I say my evening prayers?'

To my great surprise, he collapsed with laughter. 'You know, I had a mental image of you and your husband getting ready for bed, and you suddenly kneeling down to pray in the middle of that,' he said.

Wise old man that he was, he did not attempt to give me a recipe for 'praying in a marriage with a non-believer,' but he did hint that maybe I was worrying unnecessarily.

I am sure he was right that worrying was not going to help. On the other hand, there clearly was a problem. In her book about family spirituality, *Ordinary Way*, Dolores Lecky writes of her own experience of praying within a family where both parents are Catholics – of morning and evening prayers, of blessing her children as they leave for school, of prayers for special occasions.

> The practise of family prayer best begins, I believe, when children are infants. Just as babies know they can rely on their parents for food and affection, they can come to expect that praise,

thanksgiving, petition – that explicit recognition of the Holy One
– will be in their family. The very first step of common prayer in
the life of a young family is for the wife and husband to be
together, at some time in the day, in some kind of prayer.[1]

None of this was going to be possible for us. As I prepared for
marriage, I wondered not only 'How am I going to pray?' but also
'Is there any way at all that we can share prayer?'

My mother had said 'goodnight prayers' with us while we were
small and that is the only kind of 'family prayer' that I had been
familiar with. In friends' houses I had also come across the practice of saying 'grace' at meals. If I had married a believer, I think I
would have tried to introduce 'grace' in our home, even though I
have never grown fully comfortable with the practice, perhaps
because I did not grow up with it. In a marriage such as mine it
would, in addition, have emphasised a fundamental difference
within the family every time we sat down to a meal, which I do not
think would have been reasonable.

I once discussed this with a friend who said that he always said
'Thank you,' however briefly, when he sat down to a meal.

'I do it silently when I'm with people it might embarrass,' he
said, 'but I say "grace" aloud, when I'm with people who feel comfortable with it.' This seems to me a balanced approach and one
which I have tried to follow.

As it was, the only kind of 'family prayer' I tried to introduce
was 'goodnight prayers' with our daughter. I was very touched that
my husband always came and sat in on these and it is the closest we
have ever come to praying as a family. It would not have occurred
to me to ask him to 'say prayers' with our daughter when I was not
there, but one evening I got back late, having left the house before
our daughter's bedtime. He said, 'I have said her prayers with her.'
My husband had made a commitment to try to bring her up as a
Catholic and he was taking it seriously.

He made another contribution to the bedtime routine which
was entirely his own. Night after night, over many years, he told
our daughter stories, as a private ritual between the two of them.
On the occasions when he was away and our daughter asked me

for a story I am afraid that she did not think very much of my attempts. Story telling is my husband's gift.

As our daughter grew older, she got less and less interested in 'goodnight prayers', to the extent that I felt it was better to say to her, 'You are now big enough to say your own prayers.' I do not think she said them, but I did not want to force her.[2]

And the bedtime stories? I think she grew out of them, rather than tired of them. But she still sometimes says. 'Do you remember when you told me all those stories, Dad?'

Going to church

Delia Smith, the British television cook and writer on spirituality, once gave a talk on prayer at the University of East Anglia for which I will always be grateful to her. She particularly touched me, when she mentioned how her non-Catholic (I think she said non-believing) husband had driven her to innumerable churches over the years, so that she could get to mass. I seem to remember that she said something about 'blessing all such husbands'.

One husband I know of finds a nice bar, where his wife joins him after mass! My husband tends to walk around, finding interesting shops for us to look at together later on. The number of strange towns in which he has inspected the shopping possibilities, particularly before I could drive, is large!

On one such occasion the churches of three or four different denominations were dotted along the same street. When I came out of church, my husband said, 'It was incredible, seeing this straggle of people going into each church. Does it have to be like that?'

The local Catholic Church where we live is within cycling distance (just!). I took our daughter to church on the back of my bicycle for her first few years, until I learnt to drive. One morning she did not want to go, so I set out, rather missing the small girl on the seat behind me. When I was almost at the church, my husband caught up with me in the car, bearing a small girl who had changed her mind.

I think she enjoyed church for a time, especially once I started doing classes with some of the children during the first part of mass and she could make a contribution with drawing and ideas for displays. But the time came when she was no longer interested, at any rate in what I was able to provide.

'Mum, can't we go and sit on the grass sometimes?' she said. 'It would be much more fun.' It probably would have been, but at the time I felt I had a 'programme' to get through, and that would not have been so easy outside.

When someone else took over the classes, and we were in church for the whole service, her interest grew even less, until one day she said, 'Mum, when can I stop going to church?'

I mentioned this to my husband. He looked tense. I think he was expecting me to ask him to help 'persuade' her to go on going to church. Instead I said, 'I think it's time for her to decide whether she wants to go to church or not, don't you?' I don't remember her making any particular comment when we told her, but later that evening, when she was getting ready for bed, she looked at her bare arm and said. 'Look how beautifully my muscles are put together, how my hand works. I wonder how much people will know about my arm in twenty years' time. Incredible that a lump of meat can work like this, that my fingers can move when I decide to move them . . . '

It must have impressed me, because I recently discovered the notes where I had written down her words that night. It was a long time since she had shared that kind of thing with me.

The *Directory of Children's Masses* gives advice and instructions about how to celebrate masses attended by children. It is particularly gentle and sensitive to the needs of small, and older, children and speaks of giving them the opportunity to go to mass with the family *'when they so wish'*. It also explores the way in which prayer at home can help prepare children for a fuller sharing when, later on, they do take part in the eucharistic liturgy.[3]

'When they so wish': in retrospect, I wish I had been much more flexible about taking our daughter to church and more sensitive to how she felt. I thought that if I complied with the rules, religion would somehow 'take'. On the few occasions when I allowed her not to go I was afraid that I might not have done all I could to bring her up as a Catholic. When she finally stopped going to mass, it hurt very much. But I also have to admit that I did spend a lot of time thinking about what I would say, if people asked me why she no longer came to church. I had wanted to try to share my faith with her and I had genuinely believed that it was right to take her to church every Sunday, if at all possible, but the part of me that was so concerned with what other people would say, if I did not bring her to church, is one that I am far from proud of.

It is a consolation to remember some words from my priest friend – the same one who had heard me express my fears about 'How will I say my evening prayers?' shortly before I married. Now I was expressing regrets about some situation where, with hindsight, I felt I had behaved inadequately. 'Could you actually have done anything else *at the time*?' he said.

My prayer

I do not think anyone ever taught me how to pray, but I did learn something from watching other people pray. For instance, there were some people I admired who used to sit quietly praying after mass, or in front of the tabernacle[4] at other times, and I thought I should try to pray that way too. No one told me what was supposed to happen during silent prayer, but I can remember a comment to the effect that 'that kind of prayer could not be forced'. I wondered: 'What could not be forced?' Even so, I somehow acquired the conviction that this was a good way to pray and I persevered.

There is a collection of Psalms and other readings mainly from Scripture (known as the *Prayer of the Church*) which forms the basis of monastic prayer in the Catholic Church. Increasingly, in a simplified version, it is being used by lay people. There are prayers for different seasons and for different times of the day, for morning, evening and night prayer. I had been introduced to the 'night prayer' at youth camps in my teens and this was a form of prayer that I liked. When a rather prim and proper aunt of mine asked me what I wanted for Christmas one year, I thought, 'If I ask her for the *Prayer of the Church*, she can't possibly think it is an unsuitable choice!' I got the book and I do not know how I would live without it now!

Trying to pray silently and praying the Psalms and readings from the *Prayer of the Church*, were the two 'hinges' of my 'own' prayer when I got married. Before then, I had been used to regular contact with others, especially in my research work at Keele and attending lectures in Copenhagen. When we moved to Wales, I still had my exams to prepare for in Copenhagen and it would have been helpful, and given me some human contact, if I had been able to attend lectures in Swansea. There was a snag, however. 'You will have to wait a year before you can apply for a grant,' I was told. As we had put most of our money into buying a house, we decided that I would have to spend the year preparing for the final exams for my (rather protracted!) Danish MA by myself. During this year the *Prayer of Church* came to provide a structure to my day without which I would have been unlikely to survive.

To begin with, during that first year of marriage, there were days when I just sat staring at a cookery book, *not* deciding what we were going to have for dinner! I do not think I consciously decided that a scheme of regular prayer was the way to help shape my day, but as I began to use the opportunities provided by my *Prayer of the Church*, I found that both work and prayer fell into place. I also realised that if I had an 'appointment' with the Lord at 12.00 o'clock, I could not spend the morning moping around.

I was discovering what others in 'solitary' situations had found out before me – a solitary needs a fixed programme.[5] This applies to people in extreme situations such as imprisonment or solitary confinement, as well as to those who voluntarily retreat from 'the world' (for example, some members of religious orders). It also applies to the growing number of people who, for a variety of reasons, live or work alone. Fr Columba Cary–Elwes mentions the retired, the widowed and the unemployed. I would add all those who work from home: at the end of a computer link, or simply writing or producing something at home.

The *Prayer of the Church* gave me much more than a structured day. I knew that these prayers were not just my prayers, but were prayed by other people, members of religious orders, clergy and lay people too, praying at the same time. This knowledge gave me strength. It gave me community.[6]

The year passed. I finished my Danish MA and, at last, was able to register for a PhD. This meant working in a research room with others and a small amount of teaching too. I had regular human contact again and I made friends. There were some evenings when I was late meeting my husband, because someone had been sharing their story with me and I felt I could not break off at a critical point. I told my husband that this happened sometimes and asked him, 'Do you mind?'

'Of course not,' he said.

I cannot now remember how I prayed during these years, though I must have had less time. What stands out for me is the exchange with other people which happened then, the listening and the sharing, of myself too.

When our daughter was born, I returned to some of the habits of prayer I had learnt during the year when I was working at home, on my own. I discovered night-time prayer – literally! Getting up in the night to feed the baby was one aspect of motherhood that I had not been looking forward to! I will not pretend that I found it easy to get up and some nights I felt more dead that alive. The great surprise of these nightly 'appointments' with my daughter was that they turned into prayer time too. I took to praying part of the 'midnight' prayer of the Church while I was feeding her and again I was aware that I was part of a praying community. I thought of the members of religious orders who get up at night to pray, but Clare Richards has reminded me that there is another community around at that time: all the mothers (and fathers too) who are up feeding and caring for their children.

> I know the members of some religious orders get up at night to praise God in the Prayer of the Church. We night-time mums and dads make quite a community of prayer too.[7]

For me this was precious time spent in the silence and peace of the night. It was also a time when I felt particularly close to my daughter. It was the time of her first smile.

The summer when our daughter was born was very hot. I spent a lot of time sitting in the garden, especially during her midday sleep. resting and recovering after a caesarean section. Out of vague interest I had borrowed the Life of the sixteenth-century mystic St Teresa of Avila and read it during my siesta. To my surprise I found that I could hardly put it down. For the first time in my life I was reading a description of what contemplative prayer *felt* like, or could feel like, written by a sensible and practical woman – who was also a Doctor of the Church.[8] (Teresa uses imagery from gardening, for instance, to describe what happens in prayer.) In its early stages of development, I could recognise what St Teresa was talking about. 'So prayer is real,' I thought, 'and all those years just "sitting" have not been for nothing.' I had been learning to pray.

Prayer and discovering a beautiful new baby are the two things that I immediately think of when I remember those first few months of my daughter's life. I seemed to spend a lot of time sitting in the garden, a lot of time in peaceful prayer at night. But there was very little energy left for anything or anyone else. Some nights I hardly slept and there were days when I wondered if I would ever be able to *think* again.

One evening we went out to see friends. At 9.30 I felt so tired that I whispered to my husband, 'Do you think it's time to go home?'

'Not yet!', he said. There must have been times during this period when he felt he was married to a zombie.

With an active toddler around, I discovered that there was less opportunity to pray for extended periods. So I found myself using 'scraps' of time. I might not have half an hour together, but I did have the odd five minutes. I once talked to a Carmelite about the question of how much time to spend in prayer and he said that it took about fifteen minutes for distractions to subside and that therefore it was better to have half an hour together. Most of the time, now, I did not have fifteen minutes, let alone half an hour, but

I found that God was there during what little time I had, waiting for me.

As our daughter went to school, my opportunities for prayer extended. Working from home once again I found that I could fit work and prayer together in a regular pattern during the day. I was putting the lessons I had learnt during my first year of marriage to good use.

Not so long ago there was a television programme about the churches and their congregations in my area and someone suggested me as a 'possible' for an interview. A researcher arranged a preliminary interview: 'How do you spend your day?' she asked. I explained that, unless I had to go out for meetings, I began every day with a period of prayer.

'I don't think I would be able to do my work without it,' I said. 'You see, I don't commute – I have that time to pray.' This was something I had not thought about before: not commuting gives me time that many others do not have.

The 'real' television interview did not happen, but I am grateful for what I learnt during the 'preliminary'.

I was forcefully reminded that life is not like that for most people, when a deeply committed Catholic asked me to arrange an afternoon of prayer for a group at her church, 'Please, not too much silence,' she said. 'Most of us are so tired that we fall asleep if we sit down for too long!' She was speaking of people trying to juggle a job, a growing family and giving religious instruction to a group of children at the weekend.

I have often felt lonely working alone. I miss having 'colleagues' nearby, but what she said made me feel privileged. Whatever difficulties my work situation entails, it gives me the time and the space to pray.

And my husband . . . ?

The time and space to pray is time and space my husband cannot easily share. He knows that I spend time in prayer and when we are both working at home, he sometimes comes into the study to get something during my prayer time. This is not an occasion for awkwardness. He just gets what he needs and leaves as quietly as he came.

On Saturdays when we are both at home doing the various domestic jobs around the house, I sometimes sneak away for a short prayer after we have finished. On one occasion he said, 'I did not know where you were!'

'Have I spent too long', I wondered, 'or did I just get the timing wrong?' There is a time and place for everything, including prayer. Fr Columba Cary–Elwes comments on exactly this situation when he says that, important though it is to pray, it is equally important for a married couple to spend time with each other, to talk or just to relax together. For one partner to cut short these precious shared moments in order to pray alone would be a total misunderstanding of what prayer is all about.[9]

When I pray at home I go into a separate room, alone. If there are other people in the house, I try to do this when I am sure that I will not be missed (though I obviously do not always get it right!). But just as I am aware of the people I love, when we are apart, so I am aware (or try to be) of the presence of God when I am not specifically at prayer.

Seeing something beautiful often moves me to a brief 'turning to God'. Appreciation of beauty is something that I share with my husband.

'You've got to come and look at the stars,' he said one evening, when we were on holiday in Sweden, 'they're wonderful!'

And they were. We had rented a cottage in the woods with no other habitation nearby, so there were no lights of any kind, just the stars – and the glow of the wood fire from our cottage. That clear night in September it was as if we were seeing the stars for the first time. The milky way – Orion – starlight.

We spent a long time, just silently gazing, together. '[He] fixes the number of the stars; he calls each one by its name,'[10] I thought, but it was only because my husband noticed them that I saw them at all.[11]

While writing this chapter, I came across a passage from Fr John Main's book *Word into Silence*.

> Meditation is a learning process. It is a process of learning to pay attention, to concentrate, to attend. W. H. Auden made the point well when he said that schools were places that should be teaching the spirit of prayer in a secular context. This they would do, he maintained, by teaching people how to concentrate fully and exclusively on whatever was before them, be it poem, picture, maths problem, or leaf under a microscope, and to concentrate on these for their own sake. By the 'spirit of prayer', he meant selfless attention.[12]

My husband is light-years ahead of me in this. That his 'attention' is wholly secular does not make it less valuable. It is a warped Christianity which sees some activities as good and holy, and others as being less important.

Cardinal Hume has spoken about this.

> It is important to remember the value of what we do each day. If we are aware of this then we escape from the trap of seeing some activities as spiritually worthwhile (such as attendance in church or prayer) and others as entirely secular with no relationship to God, save to avoid displeasing him by sin.[13]

It seems to me that there is a link between this constant attention and faithfulness to daily tasks and an appreciation of beauty. Cardinal Hume speaks movingly of beauty as a way to God.

> The music that charms the ear, the beauty of a landscape or a person that pleases the eye, the glass of wine that delights the palate – these are all 'shafts of the glory of God', reminding us of his beauty which they mirror.[14]

On the importance of beauty as a pointer to the Creator, Cardinal Hume says 'bad' pleasures are 'pleasures snatched by unlawful act. It is the stealing of the apple that is bad, not the sweetness.'[15]

This marvelling at beauty, at the world around us (which is also seeking truth), is, in my view, the beginning of contemplative prayer. How can anyone contemplate the God whom they cannot see, if they cannot first contemplate the beauty of the world which they *can* see?

On the other hand, an appreciation of beauty does not necessarily lead someone to God. My husband would not think of his openness to beauty and to 'how the world works' as being linked with prayer, but it is one way in which I can share with him something which is also, for me, an entrance to prayer.

Looking through a magazine I came upon a picture of furniture made by the Shakers. This American religious community of Quaker origin is committed to a life of prayer and simplicity, and that commitment is reflected in the style of the furniture they make. 'This is contemplative furniture,' I thought, meaning that it would fit in a contemplative setting. 'Contemplative furniture' seems a ridiculous thing to say (I did not say it, I thought it!), but there was clearly some quality about these simple pieces which spoke to me of God.

'Do you like it?' I asked my husband.

'Yes, some of it is very pleasing,' he said, but he obviously did not see the faith dimension which had struck me so much.

Facing a mystery

Karl Rahner speaks of a God-given faculty in all human beings, which, potentially, enables us to come to know the things of God. He calls this the 'supernatural existential', that stamp of God on human nature which makes it possible to see what is good and act on it, and which, in its full development, leads to faith in God.[16] The reason why this full development does not take place in so many good people, is, I think, a *mystery* in the true sense of that word: something which is *hidden* or *closed off*.

When my husband and I wonder together at something beautiful, I feel as if we are on the threshold of shared prayer (and faith). But I also have to accept that the reasons why we seem to move to a point which, in my view, could be the beginning of shared prayer, but (so far) not beyond it, are hidden from me. I now know from my own experience, and not just from books, that faith is beyond reason and that it is a gift which I can pray for and be willing to facilitate in someone else, but which is not mine to give. The paradox is that my husband is often the one who points out to me what I need to know in order to take the next step in my 'faith journey'. When he found the tomb of St Francis de Sales for me in the Basilica in Annecy and then retired to let me pray he was exercising, in a particularly poignant way, what I would not hesitate to call his 'enabling ministry' in our marriage.

This ministry applies to money matters, too. Since my husband is the only taxpayer in the family, he has to sign our Church covenant. When it came up for renewal recently, he said, 'I think it's time we put up the amount. It's been the same for a long time.'

'Thank you,' I said. It was only when I looked at the cheque that I realised that he had doubled the amount. That is the measure of his support.

Summary

FOR NON-BELIEVERS

My husband is often the one who makes it possible for me to pray, for instance by finding the Roman Catholic church in a strange place or by noticing a beautiful sight which inspires me to prayer and by respectfully 'letting' me pray. He fully supported my attempt to bring up our daughter as a Catholic, but was relieved when I suggested that we should not force her to continue going to church after she had lost interest.

There are secular equivalents of prayer, at which my husband excels, such as bedtime stories with a child or concentrating fully on the task in hand as a kind of meditation. These are gifts which I appreciate very much and which have helped me with my prayer, as has our joint appreciation of beautiful things. At such moments I feel that we sometimes reach the threshold of prayer together.

FOR BELIEVERS

Before our marriage I was worried about how to pray at home once we were married, but this has not proved a problem, though it has required sensitivity to 'times and place' on my part and I have not always got this right. The most difficult aspect of prayer in my marriage has been 'family prayer' which seems virtually impossible when one partner does not believe in God.[17]

I have been all the more moved by my husband's saying bedtime prayers with our daughter when I was away and by his support of my wish to take her to church. My husband has often pointed out the next step in my faith journey and by his respectful, encouraging and clear-sighted attitude, he exercises an 'enabling ministry' within our marriage.

FOR CLERGY

The loyal support of the non-believing partner is a great help for the believer in practising the faith, in trying to bring up children as Christians and in continuing and developing a pattern of personal prayer. In all these respects it is particularly important to try to strike a balance between faithfulness to God and to living the faith – and to being available to one's partner and being gentle and flexible about introducing children to the practice of going to mass. Through our shared appreciation of beauty I feel that we sometimes reach the threshold of shared prayer, without ever crossing it. This has made me all the more aware of the nature of faith, as a mystery and a gift, which I must pray for and try to foster, but which it is not in my power to create.

CHAPTER EIGHT

Growing Together II

I was a stranger and you made me welcome . . .

Mt 25:35

All guests who come should be welcomed like Christ . . .

St Benedict[1]

While my husband and I were learning to walk together along a shared path, both professionally and in our household, we were also moving to new terrain. For myself, I was learning to pray in this setting and exploring possible areas of sharing my faith. In these first years of marriage, the patience we had learnt through making things and trying to understand each other's worlds and our early travels together could now be used in more ambitious travel and in meeting others on our path.

Higher mountains?

After walking holidays in the UK and Austria, we decided that we would like to go somewhere different, a little less crowded and 'developed'. We went to the Julian Alps where the Austrian, Italian and (then) Yugoslavian borders meet. Here we could walk further and higher than we had before, often in a landscape that can have changed little in the last few hundred years. Cattle were kept on the ground floor of some of the farm houses, there were sickles for sale in the local hardware store (not for the tourists!) and one day, when we were walking up the slopes, we came across a weather-beaten woman loading hay on to an oxcart. It seemed to me, then, that there was just her and us in the whole world. We greeted her as we passed, but she only looked at us briefly and got on with her work. Tourists were a footnote on this eternal landscape.

Many of the lower slopes were wooded and we walked some of them during the first week of our holiday. There was a clearing on one of the slopes where a path turned left, leading up higher. 'SPIK' it said on the signpost. I think it said four or five hours to this peak. 'That's a bit far for us to go in one day,' my husband said. 'We'd certainly need fine weather, there's no shelter up there.'

'But it would be lovely to try,' I said. 'It would feel like a real achievement.'

'All right, let's hope we get a fine day next week.'

The following week began with lots of heavy showers, it did not look promising. On the last possible day for the walk, the weather still did not look brilliant. We set out and would decide how much further to go when we reached the path in the woods. Feeling quite energetic we got to the left turn as the sun was coming out, so we just looked at each other and turned left, towards Spik.

It was a long climb. The waymarks pointed us across little scrambles that certainly demanded more of me than before. As we got higher, the vegetation grew sparser, we were on coarse scree, and still the waymarks painted on the rock pointed upwards. 'If we carry on much further, we are going to be benighted here,' my husband said. By now it was early afternoon and we knew that it would get dark, very quickly, at about six o'clock. So we settled for going up to the col between the two nearest peaks and looking across the razor edge rocks into the next valley. By now the rocks were bare, apart from the ice covering some of them, and we heard the raucous cry of a bird of prey in the distance (an eagle, perhaps?) I knew that we had reached the limit of what we could do that day, perhaps also of the height we could ever get to, but I felt so disappointed that I wanted to cry. We had almost got to the top, but not quite! I also knew that my husband was right. It would have been foolish to carry on, especially since it had been an impromptu trip and we had told no one where we were going and had met no one on the way.

It was just as well that we turned round when we did. We only just made it back to our small hotel in the light. My disappointment took a long time to subside, but on our return home, my attention was turned in other directions. A few weeks after we got back, I found that I was expecting our daughter.

Other people

A friend of mine once said, about the early days of her marriage, 'We had to learn to be with other people.' This was well before I met my husband and it struck me as a bit odd at the time. Once you were a married couple, it would surely be natural to be with other people as well? Now I would not exactly echo her words, but I can see that there was a shift in emphasis between the early days of our marriage, when we seemed to be growing together mainly through being with each other, and later on, when we were getting to know and opening up to other people, as a couple.

This shift in focus from ourselves towards others was emphasised by the arrival of that very significant 'other', our daughter.

In his theology of marriage the Swiss theologian Hans Urs von Balthasar likens the role of the child in a married relationship to that of the Holy Spirit of love in the Trinity. He says that when two people love each other, their mutual love must be open to another person, if their love is not to be closed in on itself and hence become a subtle form of self-seeking. Using a beautiful – but untranslatable – Latin word, he calls this third person the *condilectus*, 'our beloved'. In a marriage the love of husband and wife blossoms most poignantly in their child, 'their beloved'. In this way, the love between two spouses becomes 'an image of the Trinity, reflecting the love of the Father and the Son which overflows in the Holy Spirit.'[2]

The love of a child takes you out of yourself. Now that we had one small other person in the house, we were having to learn to be with other people and consider their needs in a new way. I will never forget the expression of awe on my husband's face when we brought her home: so intent was he on her that for a moment I felt left out.

Opening up a marriage to others, even to a child, requires work and commitment. We each had different ways of welcoming her. For me, it was in prayer, during her night-time feeds and when she slept in the garden. For my husband it was by making things for her. He made her first rattle and at his suggestion we made a sheep-skin cover for her cot, together.

When we moved to Norwich, a couple of years after our daughter was born, it meant us getting to know new people, making new friends and, for me, trying to make new contacts for my Church work.

Of course, my husband had a job to go to, but for me (as for many wives in this situation) making contacts and finding work seemed to take a long time. There was one particularly bleak afternoon when I felt that no one in the Church would ever want to use me and I could not see the way forward at all.

That evening we heard some peculiar noises outside the front door. For a while we could not make out what it was and then I said to my husband, 'It sounds like someone crying, you'd better go and see what it is.' It was indeed someone crying. When he came back, it was with a young man and his girl friend who was in tears. They had driven straight on where the road takes a sharp right-hand turn by our house and so they had landed upside down in the ditch. They were not badly hurt, but she was shocked and asked to lie down for a bit. I think in the end my husband drove them home, and we did not expect to see them again.

A few days later there was a knock at the door. I opened the door. There stood our young couple.

'We've just come to say thank you and we've brought this.' 'This' was a bottle of wine.

'Why don't you come in and share it with us?' I said.

They accepted and we had an enjoyable conversation. As they left, I thought, 'There must be others out there needing me after all!' I could not help seeing this encounter as a sign that I must not to give up – and I was right. Not so long afterwards I was asked to teach some of the children in the parish. I had made a start.

It seemed that I could not get away from having to deal with money and hence do arithmetic! During one of our first summers after moving from Wales, we went on holiday to the Lake District. There was a working windmill near where we stayed with a tearoom serving home-made cakes. After a delectable tea, we noticed a small display of goods from the Third World. 'The people who produce these goods are paid a fair wage,' the poster said. 'Unlike many workers from the Third World, they work in clean and safe conditions – and YOU can help sell their goods.' It turned out that this appeal was from a Christian organisation (but open to all who agreed with its aims) which imported the goods, selling them through voluntary representatives.

'Why don't you become a representative?' my husband said. When we got home, we sent for details.

My husband asked me, 'Do you think you could do it?'

'All right, but only if you will do the accounts!'

From then on, for about ten years, the World arrived in boxes in our kitchen about once a month. Unpacking them before our daughter got home from school was more than my life was worth. I think we all enjoyed the shapes of the intricately carved wood and stone and the exciting colours of the textiles, but it was borne home to me that these beautiful things were doing good in a quite unexpected way to the people who bought them too. When a local minister and his wife came to buy some crafts, she said, 'Isn't it wonderful to look at something like this, for once. We go to so many jumble sales!'

We made contact with others too through selling these goods. There were the regulars who called in for the odd present, or a packet of tea, and there were the churches nearby who believed in trying to establish fairer trade patterns and who felt that this was a simple, practical way of doing so.

Some of the people we got to know in this way became friends. One couple, another minister and his wife, always had a cup of tea on offer when I called. I cannot remember ever leaving their house without having talked about something real and thought provoking, no matter how busy they were with young children and parish work and sermons to be prepared. We very much enjoyed their company at meals in our house too.

In theory it would have been possible for me to travel to some of the countries where the goods were produced. In practise, the closest I ever came to 'meeting' one of the producers was one summer, when I was attempting to sell crafts from a stall. Under a baking sun, and with the help of the family and a friend, I sold very little. Some people even complained that the goods were too expensive (the producers had to be paid a fair price) and we were hot and tired and disappointed at the end of the day. When we got home, I said to my husband, 'Well *we're* not going to go bankrupt, or go hungry, because we didn't sell much today. Just think what it would've been like for the people who *made* these things!' This sale was a very small act of solidarity with people who were poor in a way we could never imagine.

Opening the door to others requires not only the will, but the ability to see and take the necessary practical steps and each member of our family approached this in a different way. I had one big annual stall in a nearby market town, which the family usually helped me set up. Our daughter wanted to put out her favourite goods, I wanted everything to be beautifully displayed, and my husband asked questions like, 'How are you actually going to hang those baskets up?'

Practical Christianity

A few years ago a colleague who visits the local prison told me about a remand prisoner. He had turned up at the weekly mass held in the prison, but was unable to communicate with anyone. He did not speak English (or any other language known to those at mass). My colleague found out from the prison authorities that the man was Danish and so she asked me, 'Would you mind going to the Saturday mass at the prison to try to talk to him?' It was a fairly early morning mass and, in any case, 'Saturday is family time.' But I felt bad about this man having no one to talk to, so I broached the subject with my husband, who said, 'Well, I don't mind you going sometimes. The real problem might be you getting up in time!'

As it turned out, the man was not a regular mass-goer and it was possible to visit him at other times during the week, so in the end that was what I did. I think this was the right decision, but my husband had been quite right to point out that, in this case, my initial 'consideration for the family' had really meant (excessive) consideration for myself.

Before I started visiting the prisoner, I had been very worried about what to say to him. 'How do I keep a conversation going for half an hour?', I thought. I will not pretend that it was always easy (I sometimes wished that I knew something about football!), but I discovered that he was a parent, like myself, that he lived alone with his children and that he missed them very much. While he was in prison, his mother had been looking after them and he was hoping that she would be able to come to the UK to visit him with the children, so I offered to find out about cheap accommodation. When I mentioned this to my husband, he at once pointed out the details about a cheap local hotel. So it was my husband's information that I took to the prison at my next visit and it was worth doing, even though the visit from Denmark did not in fact come off. 'That was very nice of your husband,' the prisoner said.

These visits drew our daughter's interest too. One of my more enjoyable memories of this time is the two of us going together to buy a really impressive Christmas card for the Danish prisoner (the sort you can unfold and put up as decoration). After Christmas, she asked, 'Did it look nice in his cell, when you went to see him?' I had to tell her that a visiting permit did not extend to seeing his cell! But she was interested.

I suspect that 'practical Christianity' is the most convincing witness anyone can give of their faith. It is also in this kind of service that anonymous and 'official' Christianity most clearly meet on common ground. These visits were a point of real interest and concern for the whole family. They brought us together.

Love of God and love of others

Love of God and love of neighbour go together, indeed the two kinds of love are quoted as if in one breath in the greatest commandment of the Law.

> You must love the Lord your God with all your heart, with all your soul, with all your strength, and with all your mind, and your neighbour as yourself.[3]

It is easy to think that, because love of God is mentioned first, it is somehow more important than love of neighbour (and, in the right way, love of self). It is so easy to think that spending time in prayer is enough. But if I have not taken the practical action that goes with love of neighbour, then I have not done enough, no matter how I dress up my lack of action – as I found when I had gone off to pray, at a time when I should have been available to the family.[4] It is this kind of attitude that Christ criticised in the Pharisees and I think it is a constant danger for all 'religious' people, myself included.

My husband's love of neighbour has kept calling me back to the importance of a 'concrete' love of neighbour. This love means actually going out and *doing* something, or at any rate being willing to do something. In his *Introduction to the Devout Life* St Francis de Sales gives sound, practical advice to lay people wanting to lead a holy life. He suggests that, at the beginning of each day, they should consider carefully how they can best serve God (and other people) and what particular occasions there will be for doing so. It is not enough, he says, to decide to avoid upsetting the 'difficult' person they have a meeting with that day or to express a general intention to visit someone who is sick. Before the meeting, they must think of their choice of words and, if necessary, ask someone else to come along who can help keep matters on an even keel. To make sure that the visit to the sick person actually happens, they must fix a time for it and to think about how they can best help the invalid and make it a pleasant visit.[5] The implication is that unless you make practical provisions for carrying out your good intentions, they are likely to end up as so much hot air.

After discussing the theological implications of treating love of neighbour as a kind of 'secondary' love, Karl Rahner says that

> . . . whoever does not love the brother whom he 'sees', also cannot love God whom he does not see, and that one can love God whom one does not see only *by* loving one's visible brother lovingly.[6]

This reaching out to God in neighbourly love is a constant reminder to me that there is a sense in which my husband already knows and loves God, even though he is not aware of it. It is on the strength of this neighbourly love that he – and I – will ultimately be judged. The description of the Day of Judgement in St Matthew[7] reminds me that when I 'love my neighbour lovingly', for instance by feeding him or visiting him in prison, I also love Christ in him.

This Gospel passage is therefore an invitation for me to see Christ in all others. In the section of his Rule about the reception of guests in monasteries, St Benedict refers to this passage in St Matthew when he says that all guests should be welcomed like Christ, 'For he himself will say, "I was a stranger and you made me welcome,".' Further on, St Benedict gives instructions that fellow Christians should be received with particular attention, but that all guests and callers should be greeted with great humility, because it is Christ who is received in them.[8]

Treating all others as if they were Christ is not easy, especially with regard to people one does not know, for instance those who just come to the door. There have been times when the delivery of yet another load of boxes with Third World goods to be unpacked and priced has seemed like a very unwelcome chore, and the driver just another cog in the chain of delivery. I was reminded how wrong it is to see any human being in this light, when a large delivery of crafts and tea arrived one day. I was working in the study upstairs, when the doorbell rang, 'I have some goods for you,' the man said, 'where do you want me to put them?'

'In the kitchen, please,' I said. He then asked me to sign a receipt and left.

It was the most ordinary, even banal, exchange in the world. Yet I felt that Christ had come to deliver those goods. Perhaps it was the expression on his face: 'Christ with a black face', I thought (black faces are rare in my part of the world). That brief meeting has stayed with me as one of the significant encounters in my life. I will never know if the driver of that van was a Christian or not. All I know is that I sensed the presence of Christ in our brief exchange, just as I sense the presence of Christ in my husband, albeit a 'secret presence'.[9] I know that – in a sense – Christ is present in every human being and in every human encounter, but it is my husband's neighbourliness, his anonymous following of Christ, that has shown me a pattern of practical Christian living which is a daily inspiration and which no amount of Scripture study or immersion in spiritual writers could have given me on their own.

Walking with others

Our daughter is now discovering mountain walking for herself, with friends, but for a long time she was much more interested in seeing animal sanctuaries, and when we did go for walks, in drawing the scenery. We have not yet been as high up in the mountains as we were the summer before she was born, but we have no regrets about that. Letting in other people means accommodating yourself to their needs and wishes and interests, especially within the family.

Seeing my husband interact with other people on our path, with our daughter (that most permanent and important of 'others'), with the couple who had crashed outside our house, with the prisoner who needed help and (through their goods) with the people of the Third World, has given me the insight, and the courage, to try to reach out to others, in the family, in a prison, but also to those who just 'come to the door'.

Doing such things has brought us together in a common purpose (drawing our daughter in too, when she was at home). It is not the *same* as shared belief in Christ, but I am certain that Christ is present, increasingly present, in what we do. In this way meeting others on our path has meant meeting Christ too, each in our own way, which is also our common way.

Summary

FOR NON-BELIEVERS

After some years of marriage we wanted to walk in higher mountains, in the Julian Alps. Not reaching the top of the peak we attempted was a disappointment, especially for me, but other challenges now awaited us. Our daughter was on the way. We each welcomed her in different ways. I reflectively, in prayer, my husband more practically, by making things for her – and we made things for her together too. While our daughter was growing up, the whole family joined in a (limited!) solidarity with the poor through selling Third World goods, and helping a prisoner. In such shared action, through which we made new friends too, I felt that we crossed the boundary between those who believe in God and those who do not.

FOR BELIEVERS

When we arrived in Norwich, I was looking for work in the Church, but I was discouraged by initial difficulties. Joining my husband in helping a couple who had crashed their car outside our house became a sign for me that I was needed after all and Church work began soon afterwards. That I was needed in more practical ways too, showed itself in my husband's encouragement to sell Third World goods and in helping me to see clearly the issues involved in, for instance, prison visiting. Through doing such work with my husband I have come to realise that, in most circumstances, practical Christianity is the clearest and most unifying witness to my faith that I can give.

FOR CLERGY

During our marriage I have not only learnt more about Christian living from my husband, but we have both learnt about letting others into our life together. The welcoming of other people in a marriage, most significantly of a child, is, at the human level, like the sharing of love in the Trinity. We have both, in our own way, tried to welcome our daughter with love. I have come to realise that married love bears fruit in reaching out to other people and, for a Christian, seeing Christ in them. When Christ is present, whether known or unknown, a married couple grow closer, day by day, in each new encounter with Him in others.

CHAPTER NINE

Sharing Christ When Christ Cannot Be Shared

Show forth your power, Lord, and come.
Come in your great strength and help us.
Be merciful and forgiving,
and hasten the salvation which only our sins delay.
Morning Prayer of the Church[1]

This story has no end; or rather, I do not know its end.
Margaret Spufford[2]

This story has been written from inside a marriage and I have tried
to show what it is like for me as a Christian to share married life
with someone who does not believe in God.

In his 1982 address about marriage, Pope John Paul II drew a
comparison between a marriage of Christians of different denominations and of the Church itself.[3] He likened the pain of the married couple at having to worship separately to that of the pain of
separation between the churches. In our marriage, my husband and

I live the relationship between the Church and the world. For me this has meant feeling the pain the Church feels at not being able to share its message, its *life*, with everyone.

Time running out

There is a time limit both on an individual marriage and on the Church–world relationship. A marriage ends with the death of one of the partners,[4] (though their love for each other lasts beyond death) and the Church, too, will come to an end, with the end of time, at the Second Coming of Christ. The backdrop both for my marriage and for the Church–world relationship is therefore a limited timespan of unknown length. But what I, and my husband, do within that timespan will have consequences in eternity. We will be in eternity what we chose to be in our lifetime.[5]

In a marriage such as mine this backdrop of 'time-into-eternity' takes on a special poignancy: there is only so much time in which it is possible to come to share my faith in Christ. There is only so much time in which my non-believing husband can come to know and love Christ. This can lead to a sense of urgency, panic even, and I have sometimes felt tempted to try to force the moment of grace, the 'favourable time' of belief. But this is not what I am meant to do.[6] The moment of faith, for my husband, if it is to come, will come as a gift, at a time not of my choosing.

Believers who are married to non-believers live with the pain of not being able to share the 'faith dimension' of their lives fully. (Just as in *any* marriage there is pain in what cannot be shared.) However, I have found that there are ways in which such sharing can at least be approached, for instance in the joint appreciation of beauty.

Since I am the believer in our marriage, it is easy for me to be overwhelmed by the pain I feel because I am not able to share my faith with my husband. But I do not think this pain is my pain only. I know that my husband sometimes finds it difficult to live with someone whose life is essentially oriented 'elsewhere', or who, at any rate, believes that the fruits of our life together will be harvested 'elsewhere'.

Conversion and obstacles to conversion

Living the pain of not sharing faith, whether in the Church as a whole, or in an individual marriage such as mine, does not, however, have to be an 'endurance test'. The pain can also lead to dialogue. There was a Sunday, not so long after we had got married, when I came home from mass – and burst into tears, it had been so hard to go alone. While my husband was trying to console me, I said, 'If I cannot tell you how much it hurts, I don't think I can bear it.' He understood, and after that it became easier to bear, though I do not imagine the pain will ever go away, nor should it.

After 2,000 years of Christianity I cannot help wondering, with many other Christians, why the message has not reached and convinced more people. This again leads me to ask myself, 'What, in me, is an obstacle to faith in other people, especially in my husband?'

Asking myself such questions leads to a continuing process of conversion for me, but it can also lead to dialogue with my husband about matters of faith. Such conversations have often been the source of further reflection and conversion for me. (What are my real reasons for going to mass? Why was I reluctant to visit a prisoner?)

What I do, or do not do, has also sometimes led my husband to reflect. When the mother of a friend of mine died some years ago, I felt, for reasons I cannot fully explain, that it was my special duty to pray for her soul. So I went to mass on All Souls' Day[7] on the second day of November, when I would not normally have gone to mass. 'Why are you going today?' my husband asked. When I told him, he just looked at me very seriously, clearly impressed by what I had done.

We have both influenced each other during our marriage, but I feel that I have got the better part, because I often hear the voice of Christ in what my (anonymous Christian) husband says. However, he has also told me that he would not be the man he is today, but for me. 'I have got to places I would never have got to without you,' he said, not so long ago, and I do not think he was only thinking of mountains outside England.

I am writing this during Advent, while I think about the First Coming of the Lord at Christmas, but also about his Second Coming, at the end of Time. (In the Roman Catholic Church, Advent is a time for reflection on the 'Comings of Christ', his Second Coming at the end of Time, and, as Christmas draws nearer, his First coming at his birth in Bethlehem.)

As I think about my own readiness, or otherwise, to meet the Lord, I also wonder about how faith happens and what prevents it from happening. I am not a theologian but, in a marriage like mine, how can I not think about such questions? They are, after all, at the heart of what I can and cannot share with my husband.

In a discussion of atheism and anonymous Christianity in relation to mission, Karl Rahner says that we cannot necessarily blame people because they have been in contact with Christianity, but have not come to belief.[8]

My husband would describe himself as an agnostic rather than an atheist, but he remains someone who simply does not seem to be able to open his 'eyes to see God with', whose potential for belief in God and for grace-filled life – what Rahner calls the *supernatural existential* – has not developed into fully-fledged, conscious Christian faith.[9] I know that it is not ill-will that has prevented him from believing. What, then, stops him from coming to faith?

I am sure that one reason for my husband's lack of belief has been the inadequacy of my witness, not so much in matters of religious practice, as in the living out of my faith in the practicalities of day-to-day life, especially at the beginning of our marriage. However, even if I were to become perfect in this respect, his fundamental objection to Christianity (and any kind of faith in God) would remain, 'How do you prove it?' The world of faith, for instance in the liturgy and in my prayer at home, is meaningless to my husband and sometimes embarrassing (at mass, for instance), though he always treats it with respect.

Rahner speaks of the moment of transition from *anonymous* to *explicit*, fully-fledged, Christianity.

> Perhaps it is decreed that many 'find' [Jesus] more easily when they seek Him only in nameless hope, without being able to call Him by His historical name. However, the man who has sufficiently clearly encountered Him must confess Him, because otherwise he would be denying his own hope.[10]

This is a moment which my husband has not yet reached.

The prayer during Advent (quoted at the beginning of this chapter) which speaks of the coming of the Lord (in his Second Coming), which only our sins delay, makes me wonder further about what delays my husband's coming to belief. Is it only the inadequacy of my witness, the witness of other Christians and of the Church as a whole, which stops Christianity spreading throughout the world? Or are there other reasons, reasons to do with the 'spirit of the times', with the personal history of those who do not believe, though they are acquainted with Christianity?

Some years ago I came across a reflection on this question in a study of the Benedictine life. The passage, which also deals with the Church–world relationship, stuck in my mind and I find it as illuminating now as I did when I first read it.

> In view of the tiny minority of the human family, past and present, who have come into effective contact with the Church, and in the light of the signs of the times in so far as they enable us to foresee the Church of the future, it would appear that visible membership is the extraordinary rather that the ordinary means of salvation . . . The Church is therefore much more than a necessary means for the few. It is the sacramental sign of the salvation of all, the embodiment of saving grace in history, the manifestation of God's unrestricted saving purpose. Within the huge complexity of the historical process grace is everywhere at work, giving the world a *secret orientation* to the

glory of the Church, so that the Christian community can both consciously become aware of it and bear witness to God's purpose for all men.[11]

If it is true that it is indeed a small minority of mankind who will come to visible membership of the Church, then it becomes all the more important for me to see the anonymous Christian in all good people, especially my husband, in full awareness of the presence of Christ in them. Such an awareness is at the centre of the sharing in a marriage between a Christian and a non-believer. The question I finally have to ask myself is: 'Have I done enough, that is, all I could do, to make Christ known to those around me, especially my husband?' If I have, then I need not fear that day when all my secret intentions will be revealed.[12] Even if my husband dies without coming to explicit belief in Christ he need not fear either (nor do I need to fear for him), as long as he has done all he could to do 'all that is right'.

These thoughts are a great help, but I still feel that something is missing. I have been called to this particular marriage, to sharing myself completely with this particular man, yet, because my husband does not believe in God, the sharing is not complete. There is a sense in which I am living a contradiction.

'Holy contradiction'

In telling my story I have, inevitably, focused on my side of it. I was therefore brought up sharp when the priest I discussed it with asked me, 'If it is the job of Christians to make Christ known to other people, what are non-believers for?' I was not able to answer him on the spot, but I now think that the role of the non-believer can be to question the believer and to go on questioning, as if to say, 'Come on, you can do better than that!'

I have often found that a conversation with someone who *really* wants to know has drawn something out of me that I did not know I had to give (and which the other person therefore gave both me and themselves by asking).

The writer and art historian Sister Wendy Beckett has described a painting depicting a meeting between Christ and a woman at a village well in the baking midday sun. Christ is sitting at the well (at the left-hand side of the picture), the woman is at the centre of the picture, coming towards him, with a large empty pot on her head. In the background, to the right, the disciples appear, coming out of a nearby city with their hands full of the food they have been sent to buy. Sister Wendy sees the picture as an image of our need for God (the empty pot) and she goes on to say, of the woman, that 'her need is met with demand' (Christ asks *her* for water). In this way, she says, 'God gives himself, not obviously, not in terms tangible or visible, but in *holy contradiction.*'[13]

Sister Wendy sees what takes place in this meeting as a symbol of prayer, but I think it is also possible to see it in a different light.

The description of the initial interaction between Christ and the woman as 'a holy contradiction' spoke to me very powerfully of what happens between my husband and myself, in matters of faith. (Significantly, I did not see the full implications of this passage till a friend who had read my original interpretation had said, 'There is more . . . !').

Seeing Christ and the woman in the picture, my *first* thought was that I was like Christ in the story and my husband, in his need for faith, was like the woman coming to draw water. But my *next* thought was that, yes, my husband is in need of God, but he is often the one who 'gives me God', by strengthening and developing my faith. He gives me what he does not have.

This thought took me a step further. In some ways, I am *like* Christ in this story, because I have faith (and, after all, a Christian is meant to be 'Christ-like'), but I am not *Christ*. Although I believe, I, too, am in need of conversion and I am in constant danger of being satisfied with my own self-sufficiency.[14] This applies not only to my satisfaction with the good things of this world (like the disciples in the picture), but also to the feeling that, since I have faith, I am 'all right' (and hence any encounter with my husband about matters of faith must be a one-way process of me giving to him!).

The 'holy contradiction' (by which my faith is deepened

through marriage to a non-believing husband) teaches me that, before I dare consider myself Christ-like, I must see myself as being both like the disciples in their self-sufficiency and like 'the woman at the well', in her need for conversion. I must also realise that when I am given the grace to be like Christ in encounters with others, this is a gift which I can use only in awareness of my own fundamental emptiness. In the course of my marriage I have come to see that, in such encounters, Christ is always present in *both* parties, whether both believe in him or not and the Christian is as likely as the non-believer to hear in the other the voice of Christ, in whose image both were created.[15]

Encounter

It has become clear to me that I can hope to share my faith with my husband, only by acknowledging my own constant need for conversion to deeper faith. Father Rafael Esteban wrote of his experience as an African missionary that it was only the willingness to convert as a consequence of encounter with others that gave him as a missionary the right to challenge those others to the same process of conversion.[16]

In my daily encounter with my husband I am becoming increasingly aware of how much he gives me. I am also becoming aware that it is not in my power to give him faith. But it *is* in my power to walk with him with my eyes open to the God-given moment of faith, should it come.

In the teaching of the Catholic Church a marriage such as mine is treated as an exception from the norm, requiring special permission from the ecclesiastical authorities. They warn couples like us about not underestimating the potential difficulties of such a union.[17] Yet, in the UK, as in many other countries throughout the world, the reality is that the vast majority of married Catholics have partners who are non-Catholics, though obviously not all of these are non-believers.[18]

My own experience of married life has been one of enrichment, of my faith growing stronger, because of the insights my husband has shared with me and also his willingness to speak out both about the Church and my personal life as a member of it. However, it was not until quite recently that I realised that my loss of union in faith (till now) has meant insights which I would have been unlikely to have, if I had married a Catholic. A Catholic marriage counsellor told me, 'Some of the couples I help prepare for marriage, who are both Catholic, actually feel they're losing out, because they don't get those insights from someone who is not a Catholic and, in some cases, not a believer.' Being married to someone who does not believe in God, however difficult in some respects, is therefore something for which I can give thanks. I came away from that conversation with a new sense of joy and purpose. As I reflected on what she had told me, it occurred to me that such marriages are part of God's plan too. I have been shaped by marrying this particular man and I am sure that it is part of God's plan for me that I should come closer to Him through contact with someone who does not believe in Him.

Hearing the voice of Christ from my husband is one of the joys of my life. It is also one of its 'holy contradictions', because, while speaking and working through my non-believing partner, Christ keeps calling him to faith, particularly through me as the Christian marriage partner. The *New Catechism* speaks of this, when it says that the unbelieving husband or wife is consecrated through the believer. It also speaks of the great joy which both the Christian spouse and the Church would feel if this 'consecration' should lead to 'the *free* conversion of the other spouse to the Christian faith.' The *Catechism* speaks of sincere love, the patient practise of the virtues and perseverance in prayer as qualities which can help prepare the non-believing spouse for the grace of faith.[19]

The future

I cannot impose faith on my husband (or anyone else). All I can do is to try to create the conditions in which faith may one day grow.

In the meantime, it is a great consolation to know that Christ is already at work in my husband, even though he does not know this. And I am not alone on my journey with my husband, because the whole Church prays with me for him and people like him, when it intercedes on Good Friday for those who seek to follow 'all that is right'.

Being an anonymous Christian, following Christ in one's actions and decisions, but without knowing Him, is not the same as having fully realised faith in Christ. As a believer I must try to reach out to my husband, at the very least by living my faith in such a way that I do not block his way to Christ. I have come to see that sometimes the best way of doing this is 'without a word spoken',[20] sometimes by speaking of my belief in God.

Meanwhile, like the Church in the world, I try to walk the path of our marriage, in openness and in trusting encounter with my husband, and others on our path. Christ has invited all men and women to be His friends.[21]

As an analogy with what it means to know and love God, the words of Karl Rahner speak movingly of human friendship. For me his words describe perfectly the unique friendship which I have experienced in my own marriage.

> At the point where one person encounters another in really personal love is there not an acceptance of what is not comprehended, an acceptance of what we have not ourselves perceived and consequently not mastered in the other person, the person who is loved? Is not personal love a trusting surrender to the other person without guarantees, precisely in so far as the latter is and remains free and incalculable?[22]

It is in this surrender, in love, to the 'free and incalculable' other, in which God is already present, that I have come to find it possible to share the Christian dimension of my life with my husband.

I do not know whether an 'explicit' sharing of faith with my husband will ever be possible, but openness to the future also means openness to the fact that, by doing 'all that is right', some people will turn out, in the end, to have been among the closest friends of Christ. It will then become apparent that Christians and anonymous Christians were on the same path during their lifetime. There is much pain in walking this path, because of what cannot be shared, but also great joy because of the dialogue of mutual help, which is indeed a 'sharing of Christ', while climbing the path of 'all that is right', together.

Summary

FOR NON-BELIEVERS

Church teaching speaks of the solidarity of Christians with all that is 'genuinely human'. There is thus much that Christians and those who do not believe in God can share. On the other hand, it must be difficult and painful for someone who does not believe in God to live with a partner whose life is essentially oriented 'elsewhere'.

However, what happens in the 'elsewhere' depends entirely on how life here and now is lived and this life is therefore of supreme importance to Christians too. As a Christian I have been helped greatly by the insights, and criticism, of my non-believing husband, just as the Church is helped in its mission to the world through dialogue with that world.

FOR BELIEVERS

The time available to the partners in a marriage is limited by death. The time available to the Church in its relationship with the world by the Second Coming of Christ (and hence the end of Time). There is thus a finite time during which both the non-believing partner in a marriage and mankind as a whole can come to faith in Christ. This time limit can lead to an excessive sense of urgency, especially in a marriage. However, if faith is to develop, it will come as a gift, for which the ground can be prepared, but not as a result of 'persuasion'.

It may be that only a small minority of mankind will come to explicit belief in Christ and to membership of the Church. If so, it is all the more important for Christians to see Christ in all others, especially for those whose marriage partners are non-believers.

FOR CLERGY

Pope John Paul II said that in a marriage between members of different Christian Churches, the partners lived the pain of disunity in their marriage.[23] Similarly, the partners in a marriage between a Christian and a non-believer live the pain of the imperfect union between the Church and the world. In spite of this, Christians and non-believers can share much, although the tension inherent in what is not shared can become a temptation for the Christian to try to share only the 'secular' aspects of life with their partner. However, this need not happen and during my marriage my faith has grown through contact with my non-believing husband, just as contact with the world can be an opportunity for growth for the Church. Learning about God from non-believers is one of the 'holy contradictions' both of the lives of individual Christians and of the Church.

Appendix

THE GENERAL INTERCESSIONS FOR GOOD FRIDAY[1]

   1. For the Churchk

Let us pray, dear friends,
For the holy Church of God throughout the world,
That God the almighty Father
Guide it and gather it together
So that we may worship him
In peace and tranquility.

Almighty and eternal God,
You have shown your glory to all nations
In Christ, your Son.
Guide the work of your Church,
Help it to persevere in faith,
Proclaim your name,
And bring salvation to people everywhere.
We ask this through Christ our Lord. (Repeated after each intercession).

   II. For the Pope

Let us pray
For our Holy Father, Pope N.,

That God who chose him to be bishop
May give him health and strength
To guide and govern God's holy people.

Almighty and eternal god,
you guide all things by your word,
you govern all Christian people.
In your love protect the pope you have chosen for us.
Under his leadership deepen our faith
And make us better Christians.

III. For the clergy and laity of the Church

Let us pray
For N,, our bishop,
For all bishops, priests, and deacons;
For all who have a special ministry in the Church;
And for all God's people.

Almighty and eternal God,
Your spirit guides the Church
And makes it holy.
Listen to our prayers
And help each of us
In his vocation
To do our work more faithfully.

IV. For those preparing for baptism

Let us pray
For those (among us) preparing for baptism,
That God in his mercy
Make them responsive to his love,
Forgive their sins through the waters of new birth,
And give them life in Jesus Christ our Lord.

Almighty and eternal God,
You continually bless your Church with new members,
Increase the faith and understanding
Of those (among us) preparing for baptism.
Give them a new birth in these living waters
and make them members of your chosen family.

V.   For the unity of Christians

Let us pray
For all our brothers and sisters,
Who share our faith in Jesus Christ,
That God may gather and keep together in one Church
All those who seek the truth with sincerity.

Almighty and eternal God,
You keep together those you have united.
Look kindly on all who follow Jesus your Son.
We are all consecrated to you by our common baptism.
Make us one in the fullness of faith,
And keep us one in the fellowship of love.

VI.   For the Jewish people

Let us pray for the Jewish people,
The first to hear the word of God,
That they may continue to grow in love of his name
And in faithfulness to his covenant.

Almighty and eternal God,
Long ago you gave your promise to Abraham and his posterity.
Listen to your Church as we pray
That the people you first made your own
May arrive at the fullness of redemption.

VII. For those who do not believe in Christ

Let us pray
for those who do not believe in Christ,
That the light of the Holy Spirit
May show them the way to salvation.

Almighty and eternal God,
Enable those who do not acknowledge Christ to find the truth
As they walk before you in sincerity of heart.
Help us to grow in love for one another,
To grasp more fully the mystery of your godhead,
And to become more perfect witnesses of your love in the sight of men.

VIII. For those who do not believe in God

Let us pray
for those who do not believe in God,
that they may find him
by sincerely following all that is right.

Almighty and eternal God,
You created mankind
So that all might long to find you
And have peace when you are found.
Grant that, in spite of the hurtful things
that stand in their way,
they may all recognise in the lives of Christians
the tokens of your love and mercy,
And gladly acknowledge you
as the one true God and Father of us all.

(The Intercessions finish with prayers for those public office and those in special need.)

Notes

Biblical quotations throughout are from *The Jerusalem Bible*, Darton, Longman & Todd, London 1974.

CHAPTER ONE: *Beginnings*

1. Karol Wojtyla, *Love and Responsibility*, Fount Religious Paperbacks, London 1982. Originally published in Polish, 1960.
2. Attributed to Gustave Gutierrez, a Latin American liberation theologian.
3. For this striking use of the term 'single', I am indebted to Mrs Frances Taylor.
4. I am referring only to those couples where one partner is a practising Christian (in which 'practice' I include regular churchgoing) and the other does not believe in God. I do not include couples where one partner practises a non-Christian religion and the other partner has no religious belief.
5. See, *Catechism of the Catholic Church*, Geoffrey Chapman, London 1994, paragraphs 1602–32. Marriage between Catholics and non-Catholics is treated separately in paragraphs 1633–7. On the other hand, see the *Revised Directory on Mixed Marriages in England and Wales*, Catholic Truth Society, London 1990, p. 3. This directory, promulgated by the Bishops' conference of England and Wales 30 April

1990, states that ' . . . in our society mixed marriages are more than ever likely.'

6. Cf., *Revised Directory on Mixed Marriages*, 1990, p. 3. The directory recognises that few mixed marriages are 'genuine "inter-church" marriage(s) . . . The vast majority of our (mixed) marriages could not properly be described as "inter-church".'

7. Margaret Spufford, *Celebration*, Mowbray, London 1996. First published by Fount Religious Paperbacks, London 1989.

8. *The Pope Teaches. The Pope in Britain – the complete texts*, Catholic Truth Society and Catholic Information Services, London 1982–85, pp. 185–6. This address was given at the 'Service for the Family' at York.

9. Cardinal Vanstone is quoted in Spufford, *Celebration*, p. 19.

CHAPTER TWO: *Looking in From the Outside*

1. Gerald A. McCool (ed.), *A Rahner Reader*, Darton, Longman & Todd, London 1975, p. 80.

2. A religious of OSMV (tr), *St Bernard on the Love of God*, A. R. Mowbray Ltd., London and Oxford 1950, p. 45.

3. I am, of course, not commenting on the validity or otherwise of the Onassis marriage. I am simply recording my reaction at the time.

4. A British organisation consisting of lay people and clergy who help prepare couples for marriage in the Catholic Church and who also provide an 'after-care' service.

5. Feininger (1871–1956) was an American who lived and worked in Germany. He painted the village and church of Gelmeroda many times, hence the sequence numbering.

6. *Catechism*, 1994, paragraphs 2500 and 2502.

CHAPTER THREE: *Across the Boundaries*

1. Peter Schiveller, SJ, *A Handbook on Inculturation*, Paulist Press, New York, NY 1990, p. 118.

2. J. K. Ryan (tr), *Introduction to the Devout Life*, Harper Torchbooks, New York, NY 1966, p. 239.

3. *St Bernard on the Love of God*, p. 38.

4. Margaret Spufford 'The Importance of Religion in the Sixteenth and Seventeenth Centuries' in Margaret Spufford (ed.), *The World of Rural Dissenters, 1520–1725*, pp. 7 and 85.

5. Quoted in Owen Chadwick, *The Secularization of the European Mind in the 19th Century*, Cambridge University Press, Cambridge 1993, p. 10. First published 1975.

6. Ibid., pp. 9 and 264.

7. 'Beyond inculturation', *Briefing*, Vol. 25, Issue 5 (May) 1995, p. 34.

8. Canon Brian Hebblethwaite, 'Beefeaters are the guards at the Tower of London'. Sermon at Eton College, quoted by Ruth Gledhill in her article 'At Your Service', *The Times*, 21 January 1995.

9. Cardinal Godfried Daneels, 'Putting the heart back into Europe', *Priests and People*, Vol. 10, No. 7 (July) 1996, p. 255. The whole of this challenging article invites reflection on the place of religion in contemporary society.

10. See Schiveller, *A Handbook on Inculturation*, p. 110. See also, Lawrence Cross, 'The Precipice: An Image for Contemporary Australian Theology' in P. Malone (ed.), *Discovering an Australian Theology*, St Paul Publications, Society of St Paul, Homebush, NSW 1988, p. 106.

11. Columba Cary–Elwes, OSB (commentary) and Catherine Wybourne (translation), *Work and Prayer, The Rule of St. Benedict for Lay People*, Burns & Oates, Tunbridge Wells 1992, p. 135.

12. *Revised Directory on Mixed Marriages*, 1990, p. 9.

13. Sheila Cassidy, *Audacity to Believe*, Collins, London 1977, p. 210.

14. Ibid., p. 282.

15. The Sisters of the Visitation (eds), *St Francis De Sales in His letters*, 2nd Edition, Sands & Co., London and Glasgow 1954, pp. 83–4.

16. Dolores S. Lecky, *The Ordinary Way: A Family Spirituality*, Crossroads Publishing, New York, NY 1987, p. 123. (My italics.)

17. First Letter of St Peter 3:1–2. (My italics.)

18. See Margaret Trouncer, *Charles de Foucauld*, George Harrap, London 1972, p. 151.

19. See Letter of St James 2:14-17.

20. Columba Cary–Elwes, *Work and Prayer*.
21. See Chapter Nine.
22. Jn 3:16 and Mt 28:19.
23. Cassidy, *Audacity to Believe*, p. 210.
24. *Briefing*, Vol. 25, Issue 8 (August) 1995, p. 4.

CHAPTER FOUR: *'All That is Right'*

1. Good Friday Intercessions. The full text of the litany appears in the Appendix. See also, the *Sunday Missal*, Collins Liturgical Publications, London 1975, p. 198.
2. Karl Rahner, *Mission and Grace*, Vol. 3, Cecily Hastings (tr), Sheed & Ward, London 1966, p. 16.
3. I do not propose to discuss the last two Intercessions, for those in public office and those in special need.
4. The full text of this petition is: 'For those who seek God but cannot yet name him, for the indifferent and those who reject him, let us pray to the Lord.' The Intercessions always used at the liturgy at St Mary's Abbey, West Malling are based on *The Orthodox Liturgy of S. John Chrysostom and S. Basil the Great*, SPCK for the Fellowship of SS Alban and Sergius, London 1954, pp. 31–3, 39, 94. First published 1939.
5. *Sunday Missal*, 1975. Eucharistic Prayer IV, p. 48.
6. Mt 25:38–40.
7. Vatican II, held in Rome 1962–65, renewed the life of the Catholic Church and produced an important series of documents on Church teaching. See 'The Church' (*Lumen Gentium*), paragraph 14, in Austin Flannery, OP (ed.), *Vatican Council II: The Conciliar and Post Conciliar Documents*, 2nd Edition, Seventh Printing, Costello Publishing Company, New York, NY 1984. Conversely, the same document states that salvation is open to 'those who, through no fault of their own, do not know the Gospel' or ' . . . have not yet arrived at an explicit knowledge of God, and who, not without grace, strive to lead a good life', paragraph 16.
8. McCool, *A Rahner Reader*, p. 241.

9. Ibid., p. 244.
10. William Dych, SJ, *Karl Rahner*, Geoffrey Chapman, London 1992, p. 9.
11. McCool, *A Rahner Reader*, p. 213.
12. Ibid., pp. 212f. (My italics.)
13. Karl Rahner, *Christian at the Crossroads*, V. Green (tr), Burns & Oates, Tunbridge Wells 1977, p. 28.
14. McCool, *A Rahner Reader*, p. 241.
15. *Briefing*, Vol. 25, Issue 9 (September) 1995, p. 7.
16. Rahner, 'Paul Apostle for Today' in *Mission and Grace*, p. 14.
17. McCool, *A Rahner Reader*, p. 214.
18. Harvey D. Egan, SJ (tr), *I Remember: An Autobiographical Interview with Meinhold Krauss*, SCM Press, London 1985, pp. 77–8.
19. *Morning and Evening Prayer with Night Prayer from the Divine Office*, Collins, London and Glasgow, first published 1976, reprinted 1981, p. 575. Prayer for Wednesday, Week 3.
20. I am indebted to Father George Bennet for this insight.
21. Mt 24:36.
22. McCool, *A Rahner Reader*, pp. 342f. (My italics.)
23. *The Pope Teaches*, 1982–85, p. 186.
24. Flannery, *Vatican Council II*, 'The Church in the World Today' (*Gaudium et Spes*), paragraph 44, p. 946. (My italics.)

CHAPTER FIVE: *Growing Together I*

1. St Thomas More, letter to the University of Oxford, quoted in Thomas Stapleton, *The Life and Illustrious Martyrdom of Sir Thomas More*, Philip E. Hallett (tr), Burns, Oates & Washbourne Ltd., London 1928, p. 41.
2. Columba Cary–Elwes, *Work and Prayer*, p. 98.
3. I am told that, for many couples attending marriage preparation courses in the Roman Catholic Church, marriage is (almost) 'the inevitable next step', once they have started going out together and, perhaps, living together. (Mrs Frances Taylor, Catholic Marriage Care, personal communication.)

4. This is an aspect of marriage, which, it seems to me, is often ignored and my impression has been confirmed by Mrs Frances Taylor of Catholic Marriage Care.

5. See Lecky, *The Ordinary Way*. And see also Esther de Waal, *Seeking God, The Way of St Benedict*, Fount Religious Paperbacks, London 1984.

6. Regis J. Armstrong, OFM.CAP and Ignatius C. Brady, OFM (trs) *Francis and Clare, The Complete Works*, SPCK, London 1982, p. 148.

7. Rom 8:19–23.

8. I am, of course, aware that many Christians, now, have a more positive attitude to 'caring for creation' than I had at the time described.

CHAPTER SIX: *Work*

1. W. H. Auden, 'Sext' in *Collected Shorter Poems 1927–57*, Faber & Faber, London 1966, pp. 325–6.

2. 'Encyclical on Human Work' (*Laborem Exercens*), Catholic Truth Society, London 1981, paragraph 25, p. 87.

3. This fits with the Catholic Marriage Care philosophy used in the training of counsellors: 'Care for yourself in order to care for others.' Such care is only possible when clear boundaries have been established. (Mrs Frances Taylor, Catholic Marriage Care, personal communication.)

4. Rahner, *Mission and Grace*, pp. 20-1.

5. McCool, *A Rahner Reader*, p. 214.

6. *St Bernard on the Love of God*, pp. 61f. (My italics.)

7. I had mentioned my intention to write this book, briefly, to him before and he had encouraged me, but this was the first time we had discussed it in any detail.

CHAPTER SEVEN: *Prayer*

1. Lecky, *The Ordinary Way*, p. 65.

2. There are stages in responsibility for prayer, just as there are stages

in moral development from doing what others tell you to do to taking increasing responsibility for your actions.

3. Flannery, *Vatican II,* paragraph 10, p. 257. (My italics.)
4. Where the consecrated communion wafers are kept in a Roman Catholic church.
5. Columba Cary–Elwes, *Work and Prayer*, p. 123.
6. The *Prayer of the Church* (also known as the 'Divine Office', the 'Breviary' or the 'Liturgy of the Hours') forms one part of the Church's public worship – the other, better known, part being the mass. In its full form, the Divine Office contains (typically) seven liturgies for each day. Monastic communities recite these, together, at fixed times. Thus, each liturgy 'hallows' a specific part of the day – or night. I now use a shortened version contained in *Morning and Evening Prayer with Night Prayer from the Divine Office*, Collins, London and Glasgow, first published 1976, reprinted 1981. I also use, *A Shorter Prayer During the Day: The Psalter of the Divine Office*, Collins, Glasgow, first published 1974, reprinted 1986. (Collins also publish the full version of the Divine Office.)
7. Clare Richards, 'Under My Feet: The Prayer of a Busy Mother', *The Grail*, 1985, p. 24.
8. This is a 'title of honour given to certain outstanding writers in the Roman Catholic Church because of the orthodoxy of their teaching and because of their personal holiness.' See Sister Benedict Davies, OSU (tr), *Credo, A Catholic Catechism*, Study Edition, 1984, paragraph 10.1. The edition was originally published in Germany; first English translation published by Geoffrey Chapman, London 1983.
9. Columba Cary–Elwes, *Work and Prayer*, p. 79.
10. Ps 4:146–7.
11. The whole question of where 'secular' contemplation of beauty ends and prayer begins is a difficult one. Is the openness implied in such contemplation already a first, perhaps subconscious, step towards prayer?
12. Father John Main, *Word into Silence*, Darton, Longman & Todd, London 1989, p. 3. Fr Main is quoting from W. H. Auden, *A Certain World, A Commonplace Book*, Viking Press, New York, NY 1970, p. 306.

13. Cardinal Basil Hume, *Towards a Civilisation of Love*, Hodder and Stoughton, London 1988, p. 99.
14. Ibid., p. 96. The reference to the 'shafts of the glory of God' is a quotation from *Letters to Malcolm*, by C. S. Lewis.
15. 'Transforming the World', *Briefing*, Vol. 20, Issue 9 (April) 1990, p. 152. Quoted from the address given to the National Catholic Educational Council Conference.
16. See Chapter 4.
17. For a different aspect of 'praying in the company of those who do not believe in God', see Sheila Cassidy's account, quoted in Chapter Three.

CHAPTER EIGHT: *Growing Together II*

1. Columba Cary–Elwes, *Work and Prayer*, p. 132.
2. John O'Donnell, SJ, *Hans Urs von Balthasar*, 'Outstanding Christian Thinkers' Series, Geoffrey Chapman, London 1992, p. 136.
3. Lk 10:27.
4. See Chapter Seven.
5. *St Francis De Sales in His letters*, p. 78.
6. McCool, *A Rahner Reader*, p. 244. (My italics.)
7. Mt 25:31–46.
8. Columba Cary–Elwes, *Work and Prayer*, p. 132.
9. Cf., Flannery, *Vatican Council II*, 'Decree on the Church's Missionary Activity' (*Ad Gentes*), paragraph 9, p. 823.

CHAPTER NINE: *Sharing Christ When Christ Cannot be Shared*

1. *Morning and Evening Prayer with Night Prayer from the Divine Office*, 1981, p. 25. Concluding prayer for Thursday, Advent Week 1
2. Spufford, *Celebration*, p. 118.
3. See Chapter One.

4. Separation and divorce end many aspects of a marriage, but not the marriage commitment itself.

5. See Mt 22:30 and 1 Cor 13:8. This dimension of the marriage is, of course, one that the non-believer is less likely to be aware of.

6. See Chapter Four.

7. On this day Roman Catholics say special prayers for the souls of the dead.

8. McCool, *A Rahner Reader*, p. 224.

9. Ibid., p. 220. The Editor's Note on this page states that Rahner makes a distinction between two kinds of atheism: one which has closed itself to any kind of surrender to 'what is right', and a second, more common today, 'which stems from inculpable inability to understand or accept the formulated doctrine of the Christian religion'. It is the second type of 'atheism' which Rahner refers to.

10. Rahner, *Christian at the Crossroads*, p. 26.

11. Daniel Rees and others, *Consider Your Call, A Theology of Monastic Life Today*, SPCK, London 1978, pp. 20f. (My italics.) This passage makes reference to, Karl Rahner, *The Christian of the Future*, Herder and Herder, New York, NY 1967, p. 83.

12. Cf., 1 Cor 4:5.

13. From a reflection on the painting 'Christ and the Woman of Samaria' and Jn 4:5–42 by Sister Wendy Beckett. (My italics.)

14. Ibid.

15. Of course the Christian has a message to proclaim, but he or she is not the source of that message.

16. Rafael Esteban, WF, 'Making Sense of Mission Today', *Priests and People*, Vol. 10, No. 10 (October) 1996, p. 365.

17. *Catechism*, 1994, paragraphs 1633–37.

18. In the Diocese of East Anglia where I live 'it is estimated that, in 1986, 422 of 536 marriages were marriages of mixed faiths, that is 78 per cent.' See Diocese of East Anglia, Diocesan Commission on Marriage and Family Life Report, *Marriage Preparation*, (June) 1989, Chapter 1, paragraph 1. The Report defines mixed faith marriages as those 'where one partner only is a Catholic.'

19. *Catechism*, 1994, paragraph 1637. (My italics.) Although my marriage is technically a 'mixed marriage' (between a Catholic and a Christian

of another denomination) it is, in practice, much closer to a marriage with 'disparity of cult', since my husband has never believed in God. Cf., *Revised Directory on Mixed Marriages*, 1990, p. 3.

20.   1 Peter 3:2.

21.   Jn 15:15.

22.   Karl Rahner, 'The Human question of Meaning in the Face of the absolute Mystery of God', *Theological Investigations*, 22 volumes, Darton, Longman & Todd, London 1961–91, Vol. 18, p. 101. See also, Dych, *Karl Rahner*, p. 25.

23.   See Chapter One.

APPENDIX: *The General Intercessions for Good Friday*

1.   *Sunday Missal*, 1975, pp. 195–9.